ACCOUNTS OF A CAMPUS REVIVAL
Wheaton College 1995

ACCOUNTS OF A CAMPUS

REVIVAL

WHEATON COLLEGE 1995

edited by
Timothy K. Beougher and Lyle W. Dorsett

Wipf and Stock Publishers
150 West Broadway • Eugene OR 97401

Wipf and Stock Publishers
150 West Broadway
Eugene, Oregon 97401

Accounts of a Campus Revival
Wheaton College 1995
By Beougher, Timothy and Dorsett, Lyle
©1995 Beougher, Timothy and Dorsett, Lyle
ISBN: 1-59244-048-7
Publication Date: September, 2002
Previously published by Harold Shaw Publishers, 1995.

This book is dedicated to
all those who prayed.

Contents

Introduction and Acknowledgments

The wind blows wherever it pleases. You hear its sound, but you cannot tell where it comes from or where it is going. So it is with everyone born of the Spirit.
John 3:8

In the last days, God says, I will pour out my Spirit on all people.
Acts 2:17

The workings of the Holy Spirit are awesome and mysterious. Sometimes it is difficult to differentiate between His handiwork and natural causes and effects. It is also true that years of perspective are required before anyone can see how many spiritual seedlings will survive and bear fruit. Nevertheless, even the most cautious observers recognize that the Holy Spirit is manifesting Himself in powerful ways in many parts of the world. For example, revivals, or awakenings, are reported in Asia, Africa, and Latin America. Likewise, churches and colleges throughout Canada and the United States have experienced unusual spiritual renewal in the last two years.

Some of us who were privileged to be in the midst of the remarkable March 1995 meetings at Wheaton College have been asked to offer a preliminary assessment of what happened there. Alumni from all over the world have written or called and asked if there was really a revival. Some members of the extended Wheaton College community have pointedly inquired whether their prayers for revival have been answered. Neighbors in Wheaton and the surrounding area have questions. Secular and religious journalists have inundated us with queries via fax and phone. Likewise, many religious leaders have asked us to offer a candid evaluation of these significant events.

Both of us, as well as our wives, were present at the World Christian Fellowship meeting on Sunday night, March 19, when the revival began. We both attended the prolonged meetings each night, staying until the last confession was made and the concluding chorus sung. Except for a dash home at 4:00 A.M. on Monday morning, we were continually present during this astounding visitation of the Holy Spirit. Consequently, we were rather visible during the many hours of praise, prayer, confession, and testimony. Our vantage point, in short, became a magnet for questions.

After much prayer and counsel, we decided to document the story of the 1995 Wheaton College Revival. Already in the tide of excellent articles and broadcasts, a few stories of dubious accuracy have surfaced. Therefore we move ahead in these challenging waters aware of at least some of our limitations, yet encouraged by a sense of obligation and the support of friends.

Although our primary goal is to document what transpired during the 1995 Wheaton College Revival, a secondary objective is to place this event squarely into the stream of Scripture and Christian history. Toward these ends, we begin with a chapter entitled "What Is Revival?" in which Dr. Robert E. Coleman answers basic questions such as What is revival? What precedes revival? and What are the marks of genuine revival? In chapter two, Tim Beougher traces the history of revival on a variety of college and university campuses. He demonstrates that Wheaton's revival is neither new nor the parochial domain of one college.

The 1995 Wheaton Revival is part of a larger context of revivals and student awakenings, but it is also only the most recent in a series of outpourings of the Holy Spirit on Wheaton College. For chapter three of this book, Mary Dorsett has expanded two previous publications on the history of revivals at the college.

Lyle Dorsett provides a chronicle and assessment of the 1995 Revival in chapter four. The fifth chapter contains the text of the sermon preached by the Wheaton College chaplain, Stephen Kellough, on Thursday evening. This message, "Filled with the Fullness of God," places the revival and its follow-up in the context of Ephesians 3.

Chapter six is comprised of eighteen student testimonies, edited by Kevin Engel. The seventh chapter is a moving account of how students were called to testify all over the country once the news of the revival reached the public. Student leader Matt Yarrington helped organize teams of students who traveled all over the nation to spread the news.

The afterword is written by Dr. Duane Litfin, the president of Wheaton College.

The editors acknowledge that this book is the work of many people. First of all, we are grateful to the authors for their contributions. Special thanks goes to Stephen Board of Harold Shaw Publishers, who agreed to take on this project. His enthusiasm, plus the capability and energy of his staff, have been indispensable. Likewise, Tony Dawson contributed his computer skills to the task of preparing the text for the publisher.

There is no way we could have pulled this project together without the full cooperation and encouragement of Dennis Massaro and his colleagues at the Office of Christian Outreach. We especially appreciate the way he freed his assistant director, Kevin Engel, to gather and edit student testimonies. Likewise, the Office of Christian Outreach coordinated the requests for student speakers and helped send Wheaton students to the uttermost parts of the United States.

Our chaplain, Dr. Stephen Kellough, along with his splendid assistant, Mrs. Barbara W. Woodburn, helped us keep communications in place and morale high during this incredibly demanding time from the outbreak of revival through the semester. Even as we prepare this book, they are called upon to explain this revival to an ever-widening public that hungers for everything from news to personal blessing.

The editors are deeply grateful to Dr. Duane Litfin for encouraging us in this project and for standing with the students, faculty, and staff who were deeply affected by this event.

In the same vein, we are thankful for all of our colleagues who came alongside us and our wives as we prayed with and counseled students who confessed sins and experienced renewal. Countless Wheaton College faculty, staff, and administrators have faithfully given time and energy in follow-up ministry to the students as well. Although we cannot possibly list all those who encouraged students during this time, we do thank our colleague and friend Ruth Bamford, Dean of Student Programs, for her tireless ministry.

Many area churches offered help during the revival and its follow up, but we owe special thanks to College Church in Wheaton for generously allowing us to use their sanctuary for the last three nights of meetings. The senior pastor, Dr. R. Kent Hughes, and college pastor, Randy Gruendyke, could not have been more helpful as they put their facilities at our disposal.

The praise and glory for the special week belong solely to the Lord Jesus Christ. In gratefulness to Him for this great gift, we have asked that royalties for this book be donated to a scholarship at Wheaton College for students who plan to devote their lives to full-time Christian ministry.

Tim Beougher
Lyle Dorsett
Wheaton, Illinois
1995

1
What Is Revival?

Robert E. Coleman

Robert Coleman serves as the director of the Institute of Evangelism at the Billy Graham Center, Wheaton College.

The psalmist prayed: "Wilt thou not revive us again: that thy people may rejoice in thee?" (Ps. 85:6, KJV). He recognized that the people of God were spiritually impotent; the fires of devotion were burning low; their joy was gone. "Revive us," he cried, but what did he mean? What is revival?

Many today think of revival as a series of meetings designed to whip up interest in the church. Others think of it as some kind of religious emotionalism. Yet I doubt that these popular associations of the term ever entered the mind of the psalmist.

Revival: Restoring Life's True Purpose

Revival means "to wake up and live." The Old Testament word for *revival* comes from a word meaning "to live," which originally conveyed the idea of breathing, inasmuch as breath is the expression of life in all animate beings. Hence, it could be said of the dry bones: "I will cause breath to enter into you, and ye shall live" (Ezek. 37:5; cf. 37:6, 14; Job 33:4; 1 Kings 17:22). Revival, or life, was "breathing in the breath of God." As used here, the word underscores that the source of this life is in God.[1]

The comparable New Testament word means "to live again" (Rev. 20:5; Rom. 14:9; cf. 7:9). As Jesus used the term, it denotes the change in the life of a penitent prodigal who returns to the father's house, in the sense that the son who was "dead" is now "alive again" (Luke 15:24, 32). Other words liken revival to the rekindling of a slowly dying fire (2 Tim. 1:6) or to a plant that has put forth fresh shoots and "flourished again" (Phil. 4:10).[2]

The basic idea of revival is always the return of some thing to its true nature and purpose. In terms of redemptive history, revival can be seen as that "strange and sovereign work of God in which He visits His own people, restoring, reanimating and releasing them into the fullness of His blessing."[3] By its power, "vast energies, hitherto slumbering, are awakened, and new forces—for long preparing under the surface—burst into being."[4] In the wake of revival comes life—life in its fullness, life overflowing with the love and power of God.

Not everything about this new life can be fully explained, of course. Being a supernatural work of the Spirit, there is always the element of mystery about it.[5] But one thing is clear—in revival men and women come alive to the life of God.

Personal Transformation

Revival becomes evident by the change wrought in the heart by the Holy Spirit. The extent of its penetration will vary, and there will be differences in its mode of expression, but revival is manifest "wherever you see (spiritual life) rising from a state of comparative depression to a tone of increased vigor and strength."[6]

The most immediate transformation is in the renewal of individual Christian experience. When one responds fully to divine grace, there is a wonderful assurance of sins forgiven; the heart is clean; the soul is free. Faith does not stagger at the promises of God. Prayer pulsates with the fragrance of heaven. Love fills the heart with singing, and there is spontaneous praise. There is still suffering and temptation, but amidst it all is the light of God's face shining in the inner man. Christ is real; His peace sweeps over the soul; His victory overcomes the world.

From the standpoint of New Testament Christianity, there is nothing unusual about the revival experience. It is the way a person should always live. In the words of Roy Hession:

> It is just you and I walking along the highway in complete oneness with the Lord Jesus and with one another, with cups continually cleansed and overflowing with the life and love of God.[7]

Or as Charles G. Finney explains, revival simply "consists in obeying God,"[8] which means that it is the most elemental duty of man.

Revival in this personal sense should be a constant reality. The idea that revival is a "thing of special times and seasons"[9] comes from the inconsistent nature of man, not from the will of God. Unfortunately most of us experience those times of spiritual sluggishness which make revival necessary. But if we lived in the continual fullness of the Spirit of Christ, as God desires, revival would be an abiding state.[10]

New Vitality for the Church

Yet revival involves more than personal blessing. As individuals come alive to the reality of Christ, and this experience is multiplied in the lives of others, the church feels a new unity of faith and purpose—a genuine fellowship in the Spirit.[11] For when believers are brought near to the living Head of the body, they are "brought nigh to each other in holy love."[12] This does not imply lockstep agreement on every issue, but to a remarkable degree revival creates an environment whereby sincere disciples of truth come together and minor differences are resolved in the larger commitment to a common mission.[13]

The love of Christ filling our hearts moves us to care for those whom God loves and for whom He gave His Son. Out of this compassion the dynamic for a compelling evangelism is born. The commission to make disciples of all nations cannot be ignored. In the same spirit, social concern is quickened for oppressed and afflicted people.[14] Duty becomes a joy. Love naturally overflows when hearts are full.

Society inevitably feels the impact of renewal among Christians. As the gospel goes forth in word and deed, the world takes note that men and women have been with Jesus. Sinners are moved to seek the Savior. Restitutions are made. Broken homes are reunited. Public moral standards improve. Integrity makes its way into government. To the extent that the spirit of revival prevails, mercy, justice, and righteousness sweep over the land.[15]

Human Hindrances

Of course there are human factors that can hinder revival—materialism, for example. Or it might be a cultural prejudice that refuses to yield to the new spirit of love. For that matter, any perversion of righteousness will hinder revival. And because society is infiltrated completely by human depravity, revival will always have an uphill battle.

Opposition will be most pronounced from those who do not want a spiritual dimension of life. Some will be repelled by the personal moral changes called for by the revival; others will resent its social implications. Whenever practical holiness is manifest, antagonism can be expected from the carnal mind, which is against God. Such antagonism may even come from within the religious community.[16]

We should remember, too, that there are human failings even among those who experience revival. Regrettable as it is, spiritual renewal does not make one any less a finite man or woman. Ignorance, emotional instability, personality quirks, and all the other traits of our fallen humanity are still very much in evidence. Though the revival is not responsible for these shortcomings, it has to bear their reproach.[17]

The Divine Hallmark

Nevertheless, wherever the spirit of revival is felt, attention focuses not on human weakness but on divine power. It reveals One who makes the earth His footstool and who sees nations as dust on the scales of His judgment. In the might of His holy arm, "human personalities are overshadowed, and human programs abandoned." Man retires "into the background because God has taken the field."[18] In stripping away the artificiality of human achievements, revival creates a situation where the grace of God is magnified. Christ is lifted up, and honest hearts bow in adoration before Him.

Overshadowing it all is the awe-inspiring reality of "the presence of the Lord" (Acts 3:19). This is the witness of revival which has no counterfeit—the overwhelming sense of the Holy Spirit drawing men and women to Christ and making them an instrument of blessing to others. Where this is in evidence, the world has to admit that God is alive.

Some Accounts of Revival

The Korean revival early in this century is an example of what happens when the Spirit of God takes over. A missionary who attended a church meeting during the flood tide of this outpouring said:

> The room was full of God's presence . . . a feeling of God's nearness impossible to describe. . . . The whole audience began to pray. . . . It was not many, but one, born of one Spirit, lifted

to one Father above. . . . God came to us in Pyeng Yang that night. . . . Man after man would arise, confess his sin, break down and weep. . . . My last glimpse of the audience is photographed indelibly in my brain. Some threw themselves full length on the floor, hundreds stood with arms out-stretched towards heaven. Every man forgot each other. Each was face to face with God.[19]

As is true in every genuine revival, the overflow of God's Spirit did not cease with the blessing of the people gathered for prayer at Pyeng Yang. The account goes on to say that when the men returned to their homes in the country, they took the Pentecostal fire with them.

Everywhere the story was told the same Spirit flowed forth and spread. Practically every church . . . throughout the peninsula received its share of blessings. . . . All through the city men were going from house to house, confessing to individuals they had injured, returning stolen property and money, not only to Christians, but to non-Christians as well. The whole city was stirred.[20]

The events leading to the consecration of the new cathedral in Coventry, England, in 1962 furnish an example of a more contemporary renewal experience. Stephen Verney, an Anglican priest, tells how a group of laity and clergy got together to seek the Lord. As they allowed love, humility, and prayer to flow through them, "a deep sense of the presence of God" filled their lives. Out of this fellowship came the idea for a deeper life mission which eventually involved the whole diocese. As Verney describes it:

The more deeply people were involved, the more clearly was God calling them to go deeper still, and to offer Him the obedience of their whole lives. . . . The diocese became a person, a body alive with a spirit. . . . We experienced an extraordinary outburst of worship and happiness. . . . Great services were held in the new cathedral, offering up to God every part of our daily lives. . . . We have seen reality break through, like the sun through a fog, sweeping away the pretenses. People have been set free, to become what they really are. We have begun to know that a whole diocese could be a fellowship of the Holy Spirit.[21]

A Personal Witness

There have been some occasions when I have witnessed that same sense of the divine presence overwhelming a multitude of people. Recent outpourings of the Spirit at Trinity International University immediately come to mind, recalling an even more intensive visitation at Asbury College and Seminary in 1970. But it was twenty years earlier, while I was a student in the seminary on that campus, that revival most affected the course of my life.

One morning in the college chapel, a much-prayed-for student rebel stood up and told how God had met him the night before. His tear-filled testimony prompted others to confess their need, and soon scores of young men and women were on their faces before the Lord. The Spirit manifested Himself in such power that classes had to be suspended, and convicted souls sought God day and night for nearly a week.

Very soon the unusual happening got my attention, particularly the testimonies of fellow students. I had come to the graduate school feeling quite confident of salvation, though there was little winsomeness in my witness. Hidden beneath a veneer of piety was deeply imbedded pride. But as I listened throughout that first day to classmates baring their souls, and saw their brokenness before the Lord, my self-centeredness became powerfully clear. Early the next morning, after a sleepless night,

I made my way to the altar and there, with some praying friends, confessed my sin and opened my life to the cleansing fullness of the Holy Spirit.

During the first days of the revival, the little college community attracted persons from miles around by its other-worldly atmosphere.[22] Reporters who came to see what was happening were awestruck by the magnetism of the movement. One reported, "I have never seen such happy people." Hearing the prayers, confessions, testimonies, and singing in a setting of such transparent sincerity, he called it an "unbelievable demonstration of religion."[23] Some cameramen with NBC Television had tears in their eyes as they reverently moved about taking films of the proceedings. The men representing the press seemed to be aware that they were walking on holy ground. One reporter, unaccustomed to such things, "stated that it seemed an intrusion to be present."[24]

Indeed, it was like being transported to another world—a world in which our spirits were truly free. For the most part, we were utterly honest with ourselves and with one another. The sham of superficial religion was gone. Praise of God was as natural as breathing. All we wanted was for Christ to be exalted and His will done on earth as it is in heaven. A convert of the revival expressed it when he wrote home to his parents:

> How I wish you were here. It is wonderful what the Lord is doing. I have such peace and joy I can't even express it. I can't write much because I have been in heaven for three days, eaten three meals, had about three blessings, and walked about three hundred miles telling people that Jesus saves. . . . People are coming from all over trying to figure it out.[25]

Wonderful Variety

What was witnessed at Asbury could be duplicated in some way every time there is revival. Yet the particular manner in which it comes will change. The spirit of the time, local circumstances, personal leadership, temperament of the people, and many other natural conditions combine to give each revival its own peculiar color. Likewise, the methods employed in revival may vary in different times and among different people.[26]

While basic spiritual principles are common to all revivals, so different is the way these principles emerge in human situations that it is impossible to predict their precise form. God seems to delight in surprising His people with the unexpected freshness of His approach.

We can be grateful for this variety in God's providence, for it demonstrates that He is ever seeking to make His will more intelligible to His people. Yet it also serves to remind us that God is able, when He pleases, to confound human schemes. Human manipulation cannot put the Spirit in a straitjacket. What He does in revival is by His own sovereign power, and no person dare take any credit for the work.

Revival's Key Role in Church History

No matter how revivals come, they are the high peaks in the Christian life. Whether in individual experience or in the corporate life of the church, it is during these times of refreshing that the work of the Holy Spirit is brought into bold relief.[27] Redemptive history could actually be written from the standpoint of these recurring revivals.[28] Of course, in the sense that revival represents vital Christianity, it can be said, in varying degrees, that a deep revival undercurrent is always present in the spiritual life of the church. But there are seasons when this stream breaks forth in great power, affecting many people and sometimes changing the course of nations.

This can be seen frequently in the Old Testament, but it comes to fruition at Pentecost with the emergence of the New Testament church. For three centuries the spirit of revival continued to dominate the persecuted and impoverished Christian community. However, as the church gained in worldly prestige, eventually being recognized as the state religion of Rome in the fourth century, spiritual fervor noticeably declined.

Though somewhat smothered by the ecclesiastical policies of the church, revival fires still burned in the hearts of a faithful remnant. And from time to time this smoldering flame would burst forth. There were seasons of refreshing under such leaders as Augustine in the fifth century, Justinian and Gregory in the sixth century, and John of Damascus in the eighth century. During the dark Middle Ages (roughly A.D. 1000 to 1500), the cause of revival was kept alive in such movements as those of Bernard of Clairvaux, Francis of Assisi, Peter Waldo, John Towle, John Wycliffe, and Savonarola.

The Protestant Reformation had many ingredients of a revival, calling the church back to God and the Bible. The Anabaptists especially deserve recognition for their fervent spirit of evangelism, which blazed a trail of heartfelt faith across Europe. When the church became dominated by scholastic disputation, the Pietist, Puritan, and later the Wesleyan revivals served to breathe new life upon the dead bones. From these revivals, missionaries scattered out over the world, and in many areas the churches they established have experienced great outpourings of the Spirit.

Our American Heritage

To a remarkable degree, revivals have molded the course of the church in America.[29] Peter G. Mode of the University of Chicago says that "more than any other phenomenon, they have supplied the landmarks of our religious history."[30] William Warren Sweet has characterized these revivals as "cascades in the stream of the church, recreating the main course of its waters."[31] Were it not for these seasons of refreshing during several crucial periods when the very existence of the republic was in jeopardy, it is doubtful that our country could have survived.

Unfortunately, in recent years, the experience of revival has declined. Many true disciples of Christ have kept the reality alive, and, from time to time, in scattered local areas there have been some general outpourings of the Spirit. Nevertheless, there has been no real national awakening in our lifetime.[32] We cannot expect to drift much longer.[33]

"Lord, Do It Again"

Amid the gathering shadows, however, there are some encouraging signs of awakening. It can be felt in the burden for prayer among increasing numbers of God's people; it is seen in the crowds of Promise Keepers filling America's football stadiums; it comes through in the multiplication of little groups of earnest disciples meeting for Bible study in homes and schools; it throbs in the hearts of thousands of turned-on college students committing themselves to obey the great commission. In these and in countless other ways, one can sense a yearning for revival across the land.

Years ago, after the funeral of General William Booth of the Salvation Army, the sexton found a lone Methodist preacher on his knees at the altar. Still thinking of the tremendous impact of the life of this one man upon the world, the preacher was overheard to say, "O Lord, do it again! Lord, do it again!"

As you think about the great times of revival in the past and then consider the desperate situation today, do you not find yourself also praying that God will do it again—that men and women will come forth who believe God for the impossible, and that their numbers will increase until a new and mighty demonstration of holy love sweeps across the nation? God grant that it may be so! "Wilt thou not revive us again: that thy people may rejoice in thee?"

Endnotes

1. Altogether this word is used in its various forms more than 250 times in the Old Testament, of which about fifty-five are in the Piel or causative construction in Hebrew. Some examples may be found in Genesis 7:3; 19:32, 34; Deuteronomy 6:24; 32:39; 1 Kings 20:31; 2 Kings 7:4; Nehemiah 4:2; Job 36:6; Psalm 41:2; 71:20; 80:18; 119:25, 37, 40, 50, 88, 93, 107, 147, 154, 156, 159; 138:7; 143:11; Jeremiah 49:11; Ezekiel 13:18; Hosea 6:3; 14:7; Habakkuk 3:2, to cite a few. It may be translated as *revive, live, restore, preserve, heal, prosper, flourish, save,* or some other similar term.

2. A word for revival is used only seven times in the Greek New Testament, although the idea is suggested in other ways. Perhaps one reason for the sparing use of this term, as compared to the Old Testament, is because the New Testament narrative covers only a generation, during which time the church, for the most part, enjoyed a remarkable degree of spiritual life.

3. Stephen F. Olford, *Heart Cry for Revival* (Westwood, N.J.: Revell, 1962), 17. This little book of expository sermons on revival is solidly biblical and warmly written. It is excellent reading on this subject. A comparable book is A. Skevington Wood's *And With Fire* (Fort Washington, Pa.: Christian Literature Crusade, 1958).

4. James Burns, *Revivals, Their Laws and Leaders* (Grand Rapids: Baker, 1960), 39. First published in 1909, this book is a classic in its field. Its treatment of laws observable in revivals is unsurpassed for beauty and simplicity of expression. Andrew W. Blackwood has written two summary chapters in this reprint edition.

5. In *Revival, An Enquiry* (London: SMC Press, 1954), 14, Max Warren correctly observes that true revival is continuous and changing, and therefore "any finality of assessment would be premature." With a development so "alive" as this, the "attempt to pigeonhole it is futile, for the pigeon will not stay in the hole."

6. William B. Sprague, *Lectures on Revival of Religion* (London: The Banner of Truth Trust, 1959), 7, 8.

7. Roy Hession, *The Calvary Road* (London: Christian Literature Crusade, n.d.), 31.

8. Charles G. Finney, *Revivals of Religion* (Westwood, N.J.: Revell, n.d.), 1. This volume, consisting of twenty-two lectures, has remained in print for more than a hundred years and is probably the most influential text on the subject.

9. Arthur Wallis, *The Day of Thy Power* (London: Christian Literature Crusade), 19. The author in this excellent book prefers to think of revival in terms of great mass movements which stand out in history. As to what usually is given recognition, his point may be well taken,

but I see no need to limit revival to these spectacular and occasional displays of God's sovereign power.

10. An excellent treatment of this idea is Norman P. Grubb's little book, *Continuous Revival* (Fort Washington, Pa.: Christian Literature Crusade, n.d.). The author mentions how he was shaken out "of the misconception of years, that revival could only come in great soul-shakening outpourings of the Spirit." Of course, he rejoices in the times when the church was mightily stirred in "precious hurricanes of the Spirit," but as he says:

> I saw the defeatism and almost hopelessness that so many of us had fallen into by thinking that we could do nothing except pray, often rather unbelievingly, and wait until the heavens rent and God came down. But now I see "revival" in its truest sense in an everyday affair right down within the reach of everyday folk to be experienced in our hearts, homes and churches, and in our fields of service. When it does break forth in greater and more public ways, thank God; but meanwhile we can see to it that we are being ourselves constantly revived persons, which of course also means that others are getting revived in our own circles (6).

11. Warren, *Revival*, 19–37, distinguishes between "revival" as a church-directed movement and "enthusiasm" as more of an individualistic experience. He observes that personal enthusiasm outside the structure of the church usually results in magnifying personal blessings to the detriment of the larger body of believers. Very likely this observation oversimplifies the situation, but it at least points up a real danger in revival movements.

12. John Bonar, *The Revival of Religion* (Edinburgh: The Banner of Truth Trust, 1984), 8. This book is a compendium of addresses by Scottish evangelical leaders delivered in Glasgow in 1840.

13. Genuine revival is the key to any ecumenical movement, since it brings out the dynamics of true Christian unity. This has been demonstrated in the history of the church. If popular spokesmen of the drive for church union were as much concerned for spiritual revival as organizational structure, there would be more progress in true Christian unity.

14. Revival is a catalyst of social reformation. It produces the kind of concern and environment for things to happen that can radically change human behavior and institutions. Merely to try to improve human conditions by social action alone does not solve the basic problem in society. This is the fallacy of the so-called modern "social gospel," which does not come to grips with the basic problem of sin in the human heart. Until something is done to regenerate the sinful nature of man, any social program is superficial.

On the other hand, the gospel has a clear social application, and until this is realized we have not understood its relevance to our whole life. Genuine revival fuses the personal and social aspects of the gospel. Again, a study of church history will bear out this conclusion. Contrary to the impression given by liberal theologians, many great humanitarian movements have had their roots in evangelical revivals. For example, influences that grew out of revivals gave birth to the movement for the abolition of slavery, the organization of trade unions, abolition of child labor, women's suffrage, hundreds of benevolent and missionary societies, the founding of our first colleges, and the YMCA, to name just a few.

The modern "social gospel" itself actually grew out of the mid–nineteenth century revivals, although in time the humanitarian concern has tended to lose much of its evangelical content. A well-documented study of this thesis is Timothy Smith's *Revivalism and Social Reform* (New York: Abingdon Press, 1957). J. Edwin Orr's Ph.D. dissertation at Oxford, published as *The Second Evangelical Awakening in Britain* (London: Marshall, Morgan and Scott, 1949), also brings out the tremendous social effect of these nineteenth-century revivals, as does his more recent study, *The Light of the Nations* (Grand Rapids: Eerdmans, 1965). A less extensive approach to the subject is Frank G. Beardsley's *Religious Progress Through Religious Revival* (New York American Tract Society, 1943). See also the thoughtful treatment of social concern in the context of revival by Richard F. Lovelace, *Dynamics of Spiritual Life* (Downers Grove: InterVarsity Press, 1979), especially pages 355–400.

15. William G. McLoughlin, *Revivals, Awakenings, and Reform: An Essay on Religion and Social Change in America, 1607–1977* (Chicago: Univ. of Chicago Press, 1978), XIII. McLoughlin describes these larger movements as "awakenings," or periods of "cultural revitalization" usually extending over a generation or so, as distinguished from "revival," which has its reference more in personal experience. However, the two terms are commonly used interchangeably, as I do in this study.

16. Revival has a way of making people face issues to such a degree that neutrality becomes difficult. Consequently, those who refuse to measure up may become overly critical of the movement, and even seek to counteract its influence. The building friction may eventually result in schism. Incidentally, such schisms during times of revival led to the founding of many of our Protestant denominations and colleges.

17. Because revival does release the soul from bondage, it is not surprising that excessive demonstrations of spiritual freedom sometimes occur. In this sense, as Max Warren observes, "revival is a perilous experience." But, he wisely concludes, "the perils must be set beside the perils of Laodicea. More often than not there is the choice." Warren, *Revival*, 21. For further insight on the place of emotion and ecstatic

experience in revival, see John White, *When the Spirit Cometh with Power* (Downers Grove: InterVarsity Press, 1988).

18. Wallis, *Power*, 20. For a beautiful statement of this truth, see the address of James I. Packer, *God in Our Midst: Seeking and Receiving Ongoing Revival* (1987), available in book or video format from Pastoral Renewal, P. O. Box 8617, Ann Arbor, Michigan 48107.

19. Told by Dr. William N. Blair in his book *Gold in Korea*, and quoted by Kyang Check Hon in his address included in *One Race, One Gospel, One Task*, Vol. 1 (Minneapolis: World Wide Publications, 1967), 109–11. Used by permission.

20. Ibid., 112.

21. Stephen Verney, *Fire in Coventry* (Westwood, N.J.: Revell, 1964), 24, 26, 35, 36, 51.

22. "College Revival Turns Marathon," Associated Press, *Dallas Morning News*, 25 February 1950. Almost every newspaper in America carried stories of this revival from February 23 to March 1. Some of the Kentucky newspapers during this period devoted several columns to it, along with photographs.

23. Edwin Leavers, "Impressions of Asbury Revival as Witnessed by Editor," *The Community News*, Lexington, Kentucky, I, 44 (3 March 1950), quoted in Henry C. James, *Halls Aflame* (Wilmore, Ky.: Department of Evangelism, Asbury Theological Seminary, 1966), 47–48. This book, written by one converted in the 1950 Asbury Revival, is a graphic account of the events that transpired during those days. It is interesting that at about this time, similar revivals broke out on other college campuses across America, such as Wheaton and Houghton. See Fred W. Hoffman, *Revival Times in America* (Boston: W. A. Wilde, 1956), 164–68.

24. W. Curry Mavis, "Revival Tides Are Rising," *The Christian Minister*, II, 1 (April 1950), 1.

25. Herbert Van Vorce, in a personal letter quoted by Henry C. James, op. cit., 36.

26. A running summary of the way methods are adapted to changing cultures and conditions may be found in the book by Paulus Scharpff, *History of Evangelism* (Grand Rapids: Eerdmans, 1966). This study of the historical and theological roots of modern evangelism covers Germany, England, and America for the past three hundred years.

27. As noted above, spiritual vitality seldom follows an even course. Human nature being what it is, there seem to be periods of lifelessness, times when there is only a halting response to the Spirit's appeals; then after a period of lethargy, an awakening may come. James Burns notes that the Psalms are a good example of this variation in spiritual sensitivity. At one time the writer, caught up by an inflowing wave of blessing,

exults in his strength, his heart rejoices in God, though a host should encamp against him, he shall not be afraid. But this jubilant note does not last; soon, caught in the trough of the wave, his voice cries out for help, his heart is in despair, light and hope alike seem to have forsaken him. From this he is rescued by the hand of the Lord, and carried forward in a new life of joyful, spiritual experience.

Burns observes that this fluctuation in experience actually serves to call our attention to the work of God. In fact, he believes there would be the possibility of taking God's life for granted were it not for these cycles of depression and exaltation. Burns, *Revivals*, 26–27.

28. Much yet needs to be done in this field, especially in terms of world church history. What is presently available is generally limited to particular times or areas. A rather sketchy work which has something of a comprehensive format is Milton L. Rudnick, *Speaking the Gospel Through the Ages: A History of Evangelism* (St. Louis: Concordia Publishing House, 1984).

29. The history of American revivals has been variously treated by many historians. A few of the more general works are: F. G. Beardsley, *A History of American Revivals* (New York: American Tract Society, 1904); W. L. Muncy, *A History of Evangelism in the United States* (Kansas City: Central Seminary Press, 1945); Fred Hoffman, *Revival Times in America* (Boston: Welde, 1956); Bernard A. Weisberger, *They Gathered at the River* (Boston: Little, Brown, 1958); and a more biographical approach, Keith J. Hardman, *The Spiritual Awakeners* (Chicago: Moody Press, 1983). For an excellent bibliography on revival from the Great Awakening to the present, especially focused on the American scene, see Earle E. Cairns, *An Endless Line of Splendor* (Wheaton: Tyndale House, 1986), 345–65. Further bibliographic information on revival may be found in Gerald Ina Gingrich, *Protestant Revival Yesterday and Today* (New York: Exposition Press, 1959); Nelson R. Burr, *A Critical Bibliography of Religion in America*, 2 vols. (Princeton: Princeton University Press, 1961); and Richard O. Roberts, *Revival* (Wheaton: Tyndale House, 1982).

30. Peter G. Mode, *The Frontier Spirit in American Christianity* (New York: Macmillan, 1923), 41.

31. William Warren Sweet, *Revivalism in America* (New York: Scribner, 1944), xv.

32. I am aware that some historians see spiritual awakenings recurring throughout this century, and I see no point in making this an issue. For every manifestation of spiritual renewal, including the large increase in church membership, we can rejoice. However, as I have defined revival, regrettably I hold to the opinion here expressed.

33. A realistic yet hopeful perspective on what to expect is Lewis A. Drummond's *The Awakening That Must Come* (Nashville: Broadman Press, 1978). With keen historical insight, Drummond finds encouragement in some present renewal movements, while recognizing the necessity and conditions for deeper revival in the future.

2
Student Awakenings in Historical Perspective

Timothy K. Beougher

Tim Beougher is assistant professor of evangelism at Wheaton College Graduate School and associate director for educational programs of the Institute of Evangelism at the Billy Graham Center.

The apostle Paul, writing to Timothy, his son in the faith, exhorted him, "Let no one look down on your youthfulness, but rather in speech, conduct, love, faith and purity, show yourself an example of those who believe" (1 Timothy 4:12, NASB). In the centuries following that biblical admonition, hosts of Christian young people have set the pace for older believers in terms of commitment to Christ and sacrificial service for Him. Clarence Shedd, a historian of student Christian movements, has gone so far as to argue,

> In all ages the great creative religious ideas have been the achievement of the intellectual and spiritual insight of young men. This is evidenced by such names as Jesus, St. Francis of

Assisi, Savonarola, Loyola, Huss, Luther, Erasmus, Wesley, and Mott. . . . Many of the most revolutionary ideas have been worked out by young men under thirty and frequently by youths between eighteen and twenty-five.[1]

Jonathan Edwards, one of America's greatest theologians and historians of revival, observed that the First Great Awakening had its greatest impact "chiefly amongst the young." He went on to assert, "And indeed it has commonly been so, when God has begun any great work for the revival of his church; he has taken the *young people,* and has cast off the old and stiff-necked generation."[2]

In recent years there has been a heightened sensitivity to the role of young people in revival. Perhaps stimulated by J. Edwin Orr's 1971 work *Campus Aflame,*[3] more and more historians of revival are examining the role of young people, especially students, in times of spiritual awakening.[4]

This chapter seeks to briefly survey the history of campus awakenings. This overview is not intended to be exhaustive, but to demonstrate that revival among students is not an unusual nor a recent phenomenon. While the focus of this chapter is on awakenings in America,[5] the reader should note that revivals among young people have been documented around the world.[6] Church history confirms Edwards's assertion that young people are often found at the heart of spiritual awakening.

The First Great Awakening

When the First Great Awakening hit full stride in 1740, there were only three colleges in America: Harvard, William and Mary, and Yale. David Brainerd, who entered Yale College in September 1739, writes of the "many temptations" he faced there.[7] Brainerd was convinced most of his fellow students were oblivious to the things of God, and in that apathetic environment he found his spiritual vigor slipping away. In August 1740, he fell quite ill and returned home. While there, he not only regained his physical health, but God gave him "delight and consolation in religious duties." Brainerd writes:

> I now so longed after God, and to be freed from sin, that when I felt myself recovering, and thought I must return to college again, which had proved so hurtful to my spiritual interest the year past, I could not but be grieved, and I thought I had much rather have died; for it distressed me to think of getting away from God.[8]

In fact, a few months after returning to campus he sensed he once again had grown cold to the things of God. But then, in early 1741, Yale College experienced a time of spiritual refreshment. Brainerd writes, "But through divine goodness, a great and general awakening spread itself over the college, about the latter end of February, in which I was much quickened, and more abundantly engaged in religion."[9] Jonathan Edwards adds this editorial comment to Brainerd's account:

> This awakening was at the beginning of that extraordinary religious commotion through the land, which is fresh in every one's memory. It was for a time very great and general at New-Haven; and the college had no small share in it. That society was greatly reformed, the students in general became serious, many of them remarkably so, and much engaged in the concerns of their eternal salvation. And however undesirable the issue of the awakenings of that day have appeared in many others, there have been manifestly happy and abiding effects of the impressions then made on the minds of many of the members of that college.[10]

The First Great Awakening served as an impetus for the creation of many other institutions of higher education. Over the next two decades, schools such as the College of New Jersey (Princeton), Rhode Island College (Brown University), Queen's College

(Rutgers University), and Dartmouth were founded to train ministers of the gospel.

The Second Great Awakening

In the wake of the American Revolution, the nation experienced a decline of religion and morals. College students reflected this decline, and many reveled in their newfound "freedom." Lyman Beecher described campus life at Yale in the late 1700s:

> College was in a most ungodly state. The college church was almost extinct. Most of the students were skeptical, and rowdies were plenty. Wine and liquors were kept in many rooms; intemperance, profanity, gambling and licentiousness were common. . . . Most of the class before me were infidels and called each other Voltaire, Rousseau, D'Alembert, etc., etc.[11]

Yale was far from atypical. Conditions at many of the nation's colleges were deplorable. Hoffman observes:

> The colleges of the land were seed-beds of infidelity. The teachings of Deism, with its rejection of Christianity, were almost universally adopted. Transylvania College in Kentucky, which had been founded by Presbyterians, came under the control of infidels. Free-thinkers were teaching in the University of Pennsylvania and in Columbia College in South Carolina. At Bowdoin there was at one time only one professed Christian among the students. Dr. Ashbel Green states that when he entered Princeton in 1782, there were but two professed believers among the students, and that profanity and drunkenness were almost universal.[12]

The typical Harvard student was an atheist who rebelled against authority.[13] At Williams College, students performed mock Communion services to display their contempt for Christianity.

The 1787 revival at Hampden-Sydney College in Virginia marked the "beginning" of the Second Great Awakening.[14] Four young men on campus, deeply concerned about the state of their school, met to pray. When they were discovered by other students, an uproar ensued. The president of the college, John Blair Smith, invited the four students and others to pray with him. The results were dramatic. More than half the college attended a prayer meeting in the president's parlor the following week, and the revival that began there spread throughout that region.[15]

Over the next several years, numerous colleges had seasons of spiritual refreshing. Yale University, under the leadership of college president Timothy Dwight, saw seventy-five of its two hundred and twenty-five students converted in 1802.[16] Dwight, the grandson of Jonathan Edwards, became Yale's president in 1795 and began to preach a moving series of sermons on biblical Christianity.

Soon students began to seek the Lord. When a powerful spiritual wave swept the campus in 1802, Lyman Beecher commented, "all infidelity skulked and hid its head."[17] Among the converts was Benjamin Silliman, who wrote to his mother, "Yale College is a little temple: prayer and praise seem to be the delight of the greater part of the students while those who are still unfeeling are awed into respectful silence."[18]

The movement spread to other campuses, including Dartmouth and Princeton. At Princeton nearly eighty of the one hundred and five students were converted.[19] Princeton would see other awakenings in the ensuing years, like the revival of 1815 here recounted by the president, Ashbel Green:

> The divine influence seemed to descend like the silent dew of heaven; and in about four weeks there were very few individuals in the college edifice who were not deeply impressed with a sense of the importance of spiritual and eternal things. There was scarcely a room—perhaps not one—which was not a place of

earnest secret devotion . . . so that at length the inquiry . . . was, not who was engaged about religion? but who was not?[20]

A few years earlier, in 1806, the famous "Haystack Prayer Meeting" took place at Williams College. Samuel J. Mills, a freshman at the college, helped lead a group of five students who were praying for revival on the campus. Being forced to seek shelter under the side of a large haystack during a storm, Mills challenged the others to join him in the task of taking the gospel to Asia. "We can do it if we will," he said.

He led the group in prayer, providing the impetus for what would eventually become an unprecedented thrust in foreign missions. Mills would soon play a key role in the founding of the American Board of Commissioners for Foreign Missions, the American Bible Society, and the American Colonization Society.[21] Thus, a plaque at the site of the Haystack Prayer Meeting bears the inscription "The Birthplace of American Foreign Missions."[22]

Many other campuses were renewed during this period. J. Edwin Orr notes that "Amherst, Dartmouth, Princeton, Williams, and Yale, to name a few, reported the conversion to God of a third to a half of their total student bodies, which in those days usually numbered between a hundred and two hundred fifty."[23] The following account is given by a student of the 1827 revival at Amherst:

> The most remarkable and important event of our college course was the revival of 1827. . . . The stillness and seriousness pervading the whole Institution made every day seem like the Sabbath in its most strict observance. . . . Two or three, or it may be four, of the forty in the class, (1828) did not seem to be much moved, all the rest were manifestly.[24]

Oberlin College, under the leadership of Charles Finney, saw continual periods of revival beginning in 1835. Finney writes,

"Our students were converted by scores from year to year; and the Lord overshadowed us constantly with the cloud of his mercy."[25] Rudolph summarizes the prevailing viewpoint of this period:

> The really effective agency of religion in the life of the colleges was the revival, that almost unexplainable combination of confession, profession, joy, and tears which brought many young college men into the church and into the ministry. Most college presidents and college faculties of this era felt that they—or God—had failed a collegiate generation if once during its four years in college there did not occur a rousing revival.[26]

The 1857–58 Prayer Revival

An almost unbroken succession of revivals blessed the nation from the 1790s through the 1840s. However, nearing the close of the first half of the century, awakenings had seemingly come to a standstill. Most churches and denominations were in decline. Beardsley says: "For several years, from 1843 to 1857, the accessions to the churches scarcely equalled the losses sustained by death, removal, or discipline, while a wide-spread indifference to religion became prevalent."[27]

The crisis came to a head with the "bank crash" of October 14, 1857, thrusting thousands of people into financial ruin. A few weeks prior to this, on September 23, 1857, Jeremiah Calvin Lanphier, a lay missionary to New York City, had launched a noontime prayer meeting for businessmen. The meeting grew from the six men at the first meeting to more than one hundred in a few weeks. Fueled by the bank crash, the prayer meeting grew until there were tens of thousands of people in New York City alone gathering together daily for prayer.[28]

Similar groups sprang up in Boston, Chicago, Philadelphia, and other major cities. Soon the whole nation was caught up in the sweep of the revival.

The awakening during the years 1857–58 has been termed the "Prayer Revival," "Businessmen's Revival" or "Laymen's Revival."[29] It was marked, not by well-known personalities, but by the leadership of the laity.[30] It was promoted as it had begun—not through preaching, but by prayer.

Several colleges experienced revival during these years, including Oberlin, Yale, Dartmouth, Middlebury, Princeton, Williams, Wofford, Amherst, the University of North Carolina, Wake Forest, Trinity, Wabash, the University of Georgia, Emory, and the University of Michigan.[31] Orr notes that the *Oberlin Evangelist,* a newspaper produced by Finney's school, argued that the most precious feature of the 1857–58 Awakening was the impact on the colleges, with revival having occurred on most campuses in the nation.[32]

Dr. Augustus Stearns, the president of Amherst College, reported:

> The religious community will be interested to know that in the 'Great Awakening' of the times, Amherst College has not passed by unblessed. A wonderful revival has just been experienced here. It commenced with the term which has recently closed. From small beginnings it made gradual progress, till our entire collegiate community was brought under its influence. . . . The reformation of character and manners was no less remarkable than the renewal of hearts. College discipline, in the way of restraint and censure, seemed to lose its office; order prevailed, study was attended to as a religious duty; sacred psalms took the place of questionable songs, and social revelries gave way to heavenly friendships.[33]

Frederick Rudolph, a historian of American colleges, believed it was the greatest year of revivals ever for college campuses.[34] The revival not only touched existing campuses, but encouraged denominations to begin new schools.[35]

The Revival of 1904–1908

Many people are aware of the great movement of revival which swept Wales in 1904–1905.[36] Some may not know, however, that a movement of revival began during this same period in the United States at Azusa Street in Los Angeles.[37] The Azusa Street Revival became the spark for what would become the worldwide Pentecostal and Charismatic movements.

During these years, many churches across the nation experienced renewal. Campuses felt the impact. Not only Christian institutions such as Taylor University and Asbury College, but also secular colleges and universities such as Cornell University and the University of California at Berkeley were seeing outbreaks of revival.[38]

A "universal day of prayer for students" was implemented in college after college. Students met in both large and small groups to pray for the spread of the revival.[39] And spread it did, with virtually every campus in America eventually being touched by awakening. The account of revival at Seattle Pacific College is illustrative:

> On the night of December 18, in our new Chapel at Seattle Seminary, we had a most glorious meeting. A large congregation gathered in the Chapel and from the beginning God manifested His power and glory. . . . At times, the Spirit was so outpoured as to make it impossible to describe the scene. . . . Wave after wave of blessing, billow after billow of divine glory rolled over the entire congregation. . . . So great was the power of God that the unsaved were unable to resist and a number of them broke down and commenced to seek the Lord. The meeting continued in power and interest until long after midnight, and a number were saved.[40]

Wesley Duewel tells what happened at Asbury College in 1905:

A few male students, including E. Stanley Jones, were holding a prayer meeting in a dormitory room when the Holy Spirit descended upon them. The next day the Spirit was poured out upon the regular chapel service in Asbury and intercession took over. The revival spread through the college and town and continued for days.[41]

This marked a turning point for E. Stanley Jones, as he committed to going to India as a missionary. Jones was not the only student thrust out to the mission field from the revival of 1904–08. Perhaps as many as ten to fifteen thousand missionaries went overseas from college campuses as a result of this awakening.[42]

Campus Revivals in the Mid-Twentieth Century

Following World War II, there were signs of a resurgence of religious life in America. Revivals began to occur in Christian colleges in 1949 and 1950. Fred Hoffman highlights a specific prayer meeting which preceded this period of awakening. Billy Graham, at that time president of Northwestern Bible Schools in Minneapolis, held a prayer meeting in his office, which included J. Edwin Orr, Armin Gesswein, Jack Franck, and William Dunlap. They met after midnight to pray for a spiritual awakening among college students. Within a week, a powerful revival had broken out at Bethel College in St. Paul, Minnesota.[43] The president of Bethel, Henry C. Wingblade, gave this account:

> We have had a special visitation. The Holy Spirit has wrought a marvelous work indeed on our campus and we praise Him for it. . . . I do not think we have had anything quite like (these meetings) in all the history of Bethel. There was confession of every known sin, and a cleansing of heart and the preparing of vessels to be used of the Lord for His glory.[44]

In the days and weeks to follow, the spreading flame of revival would touch many campuses across the land, among them Wheaton, North Park, Houghton, Asbury, Seattle Pacific, Mult-nomah School of the Bible, Westmont, John Brown University, Northern Baptist Theological Seminary, and Fuller Theological Seminary.[45] Newspapers across the country, as well as magazines such as *Life, Newsweek,* and *Time,* reported on the dramatic events.

Dr. W. W. Holland, chairman of the division of philosophy and religion at Asbury College, tells what happened when revival began during a morning chapel service on February 23, 1950:

> The floodgates of heaven lifted and God moved into our midst as I have never before witnessed. The Holy Spirit fell upon the entire audience and everything broke loose. Testimonies were followed by confessions, confessions by crowded altars, crowded altars gave place to glorious spiritual victories, and this in turn to more testimonies. . . . At times, the Divine presence was so pronounced that one could gather some conception of what St. Paul must have experienced when he was caught up into the Third Heaven.[46]

As campuses were touched during this time period, many "fellowship groups" sprang up. Whereas the YMCA had been birthed following the 1857–58 Prayer Awakening, the movement of God on campuses in the 1940s and 50s saw the creation of ministries such as Campus Crusade for Christ and the Inter-Varsity Christian Fellowship. These and other similar groups would become avenues for maintaining spiritual life on college campuses across the country in succeeding years.

The mid-twentieth century revivals brought forth a new generation of Christian leaders. As David McKenna observes, "In one way or another, Billy Graham, Carl F. H. Henry, Harold

Ockenga, Robert Cook, Bill Bright and many other prominent evangelical leaders are linked to these life-changing moments."[47]

The Campus Revivals of 1970

To label the 1960s in America as a "turbulent" decade is no exaggeration. In this era filled with drugs, sex, violence, tear gas, shootings, arson, bombings, the Vietnam War, riots, and assassinations, colleges and universities were scenes of frequent demonstrations, many resulting in the destruction of property. Conditions grew so bad that by 1970, several schools cancelled commencement services because of fear of violence.

That religion and church life were in marked decline was evident by this cover caption on the April 8, 1966 *Time* magazine: "Is God Dead?" The question was not only being asked by liberal theologians. America seemed to be falling apart at the seams. Where was God? Churches faced sagging attendance, enrollment fell at seminaries, and religious book sales lagged.

But in the midst of the bad news, signs of hope were appearing. Thus, *Time* magazine's last cover of 1969 asked, "Is God Coming Back to Life?"

One such sign of hope was the revival at Asbury College and Seminary during February 1970.[48] One observer describes the situation in Wilmore, Kentucky:

> While many students across America were burning down buildings and rioting in the streets, students in this college community were strangely drawn to their knees to pray. It was as if the campus had been suddenly invaded by another Power. Classes were forgotten. Academic work came to a standstill. In a way awesome to behold, God had taken over the campus. Caught up in the wonder of it, a thousand students remained for days in the college auditorium—not to demand more freedom or to protest the Establishment, but to confess their sin and to sing the praises of their Saviour.[49]

The Asbury revival began in a college chapel service in Hughes Auditorium on February 3, 1970. Following a time of testimonies,

> a mass of students moved forward. . . . There was not room for all who wanted to pray at the altar. Many had to kneel in the front seats of the auditorium. Their prayers were mingled with heartfelt contrition and outbursts of joy. It was evident that God was moving upon His people in power. The presence of the Lord was so real that all other interests seemed unimportant. The bell sounded for classes to begin but went unheeded.[50]

Classes were cancelled for the remainder of the day as students continued to testify and pray. A student wrote this account:

> I sit in the middle of a contemporary Pentecost. A few moments ago there came a spontaneous movement of the Holy Spirit. . . . The scene is unbelievable. . . . Witness is abundant. Release—Freedom—Tears—Joy unspeakable—Embracing—Spontaneous applause when a soul celebrates. A thousand hearts lifted in songs of praise and adoration to a mighty God.[51]

The revival spread to the seminary campus during its chapel service the next day, following the same format of open confession of sin and desire for a fresh touch from the Holy Spirit. The meetings lasted for eight days and nights, some 185 hours without interruption. Even when classes resumed, many students would gather each evening to continue to celebrate God's presence in their midst.[52] The revival influenced many people outside the college and seminary community:

> "I've never seen anything like it," one veteran newscaster told his television audience. Then he asked his viewers to put down their newspapers, stop whatever they were doing, and watch the revival scene which he had filmed earlier in the day. "Though I've seen it," he concluded, "I still can't believe it."[53]

As news of the revival spread, people from other campuses called to ask for prayer for their schools. Soon Asbury students fanned out across the nation to tell what God had done on their campus and in their individual lives.

By the summer of 1970 at least 130 colleges, seminaries and Bible schools had been touched by the revival outreach, and Asbury students continued to go to other schools and local churches.[54] Schools affected included Azusa [Pacific] College, Taylor University, Spring Arbor College, Roberts Wesleyan College, Oral Roberts University, Greenville College, and Southwestern Baptist Theological Seminary, just to name a few.[55]

Conclusion

Spiritual awakening often centers around young people. During each season of revival in America, college campuses have been blessed with a fresh touch of the Spirit of God. Gary Stratton, dean of the chapel at Gordon College, maintains:

> It is not far off the mark to say every missions movement in modern church history and the vast majority of the church's leadership in each generation have been the product of one or more college awakenings.[56]

This is not to say that God works *only* among the young or *always* among them. But some questions remain: Why young people? Why do awakenings often impact college campuses? Why do campus awakenings typically profoundly affect students, but have a lesser impact on faculty, staff, and administration? With a keen realization that any attempt to give simple answers is bound to produce an oversimplification, let me suggest a few possible reasons.

A key characteristic of students, and young people in general, is idealism. Douglas Hyde, a former communist turned Catholic, had this to say:

Youth is a period of idealism. The Communists attract young
people by appealing directly to that idealism. Too often, others
have failed either to appeal to it or to use it and they are the losers
as a consequence. We have no cause to complain if, having
neglected the idealism of youth, we see others come along, take
it, use it and harness it to their cause—and against our own. . . .

Young people are idealistic. This is natural to any healthy
youngster. I can only conclude that it is the way God wants them
to be. We offend against charity and justice, and against com-
monsense too, when we sneer at starry-eyed idealism. We do it
to our own loss.[57]

The beautiful thing about this idealism is that it is not simply
"starry-eyed"; it is quite practical. Young people are willing to
pay a price for their commitment to a vision. When the Scripture
states in 2 Chronicles 16:9 (NASB), "For the eyes of the Lord
move to and fro throughout the earth that He may strongly
support those whose heart is completely His," is it any wonder
that the Lord's searching gaze often rests upon a young person?
Whether it is the tenacity of a young missionary like Jim Elliot
or the audacity displayed by the Chinese student single-handedly
stopping a row of tanks in Tiananmen Square, young people are
willing to sacrifice for a cause in which they believe.

Young people in general are also open to change. Their lives are
not yet set in concrete, but are pliable in God's hands. As we grow
older, we develop greater skill in self-protection. We become more
concerned about our reputation. In doing so, we perhaps become
less open to a moving of God's Spirit in our lives.

While there is much about God and His working during times
of revival that we cannot understand, it seems clear that seeds
of awakening often find fertile soil in the hearts of young people.
David McKenna's observation is right on target:

When God's Spirit is poured out on all people, it is no accident
that the young see visions. Nor is it an accident when the stirring

of the Spirit that leads to a Great Awakening begins on the college campus. Youth is a choice time of life when special gifts are in full bloom. Never again will a person be so *sensitive* to cultural conflict, so *optimistic* about the future, so *open* to the Spirit, so *energized* for action, and so *ready* to die for Christ.[58]

"Let no one look down on your youthfulness, but rather in speech, conduct, love, faith and purity, show yourself an example to those who believe" (1 Tim. 4:12, NASB). Students throughout the history of spiritual awakening have been doing just that. And the kingdom of God is richer as a result.

Endnotes

1. Clarence P. Shedd, *Two Centuries of Student Christian Movements* (New York: Association Press, 1934), 1.

2. Jonathan Edwards, "Some Thoughts Concerning the Present Revival of Religion in New England," in *The Works of Jonathan Edwards* (London: Banner of Truth Trust, 1834, 1987 reprint), Vol. I, 423 [emphasis added].

3. J. Edwin Orr, *Campus Aflame: Dynamic of Student Religious Revolution* (Glendale, Calif.: Regal Books, 1971). A new and revised edition, edited by Richard Owen Roberts, was published as *Campus Aflame: A History of Evangelical Awakenings in Collegiate Communities* (International Awakening Press, 1994). Citations in this chapter are from the newer edition.

Among the helpful books which predated Orr's were David M. Howard, *Student Power in World Evangelism* (Downers Grove, Ill.: InterVarsity Press, 1970), and two books which focused specifically on revival at Asbury College and Seminary in Wilmore, Ky.: Henry C. James and Paul Rader, *Halls Aflame: An Account of the Spontaneous Revivals at Asbury College in 1950 and 1958* (Wilmore, Ky.: Asbury Theological Seminary, 1966); and *One Divine Moment*, ed. by Robert E. Coleman (Old Tappan, N.J.: Revell, 1970).

4. See, for example, Dan Hayes, *Fireseeds of Spiritual Awakening* (San Bernardino, Calif.: Here's Life Publishers, 1983); David L. McKenna, *The Coming Great Awakening* (Downers Grove, Ill.: InterVarsity Press, 1990); and Alvin L. Reid, "The Zeal of Youth: The Role

of Students in the History of Spiritual Awakening," in *Evangelism for a Changing World*, ed. by Timothy K. Beougher and Alvin L. Reid (Wheaton, Ill.: Harold Shaw Publishers, 1995), 233–48.

5. There is no consensus among historians when it comes to dating spiritual awakenings in America. For the purpose of this paper, the following rough divisions will be followed: The First Great Awakening, 1730s–40s; The Second Great Awakening, 1780s–1830s; The Prayer Revival of 1857–58; The Revival of 1904–08; mid–twentieth century revivals; and the revivals of 1970.

6. In addition to Orr, *Campus Aflame*, see: Earle E. Cairns, *An Endless Line of Splendor: Revivals and Their Leaders from the Great Awakening to the Present* (Wheaton: Tyndale House, 1986); Wesley Duewel, *Revival Fire* (Grand Rapids: Zondervan, 1995); and David L. McKenna, *The Coming Great Awakening*.

7. "The Life and Diary of David Brainerd," in *The Works of Jonathan Edwards* (London: Banner of Truth Trust, 1834, 1987 reprint), 2:320.

8. Ibid.

9. Ibid.

10. Ibid.

11. *Autobiography, Correspondence, etc. of Lyman Beecher*, edited by Charles Beecher (New York: Harper, 1864), vol. 1, 43. See also Benjamin Silliman, *A Sketch of the Life and Character of President Dwight* (New Haven, Conn.: Maltby, Goldsmith, 1817), 19.

12. Fred W. Hoffman, *Revival Times in America* (Boston: Wilde Company, 1956), 66.

13. Samuel Eliot Morison, *Three Centuries of Harvard, 1636–1936* (Cambridge, Mass.: Harvard Univ. Press, 1936), 185.

14. Benjamin R. Lacy, Jr., *Revivals in the Midst of the Years* (Richmond, Va.: John Knox Press, 1943), 68.

15. Charles Thompson, *Times of Refreshing: A History of American Revivals from 1740 to 1877, With their Philosophy and Methods* (Chicago: L. T. Palmer, 1877), 79.

16. Orr, *Campus Aflame*, 26.

17. *Autobiography, Correspondence, etc. of Lyman Beecher*, 1:43.

18. George P. Fisher, *Life of Benjamin Silliman* (1866), 1, 83, cited in Ralph Henry Gabriel, *Religion and Learning at Yale: The Church of Christ in the College and University, 1757–1957* (New Haven, Conn.: Yale Univ. Press, 1958), 72.

19. Cairns, *An Endless Line of Splendor*, 92.

20. Ashbel Green, *A Report to the Trustees of the College of New-Jersey* (New Haven: Hudson & Woodward, 1815), 4.

21. For a concise account of Mills's time at Williams College and his subsequent influence on global missions, see Keith J. Hardman, *The Spiritual Awakeners: American Revivalists from Solomon Stoddard to D. L. Moody* (Chicago: Moody Press, 1983).

22. *The One Hundreth Anniversary of the Haystack Prayer Meeting* (Boston: American Board of Commissioners for Foreign Missions, 1907), 4.

23. Orr, *Campus Aflame*, 41.

24. Letter of A. Tobey, class of 1828, cited in W. S. Tyler, *History of Amherst College During its First Half Century 1821–1871* (Springfield, Mass.: Clark W. Bryan and Company, 1873), 199.

25. *The Memoirs of Charles G. Finney: The Complete Restored Text,* ed. by Garth M. Rosell & Richard A. G. Dupuis (Grand Rapids: Zondervan, 1989), 405–06.

26. Frederick Rudolph, *The American College and University: A History* (New York: Alfred A. Knopf, 1962), 77–78. Rudolph mentions that at Amherst there was a revival at least every four years between 1823 and 1870. See Rudolph, 84.

27. Frank G. Beardsley, *Religious Progress Through Religious Revivals* (New York: American Tract Society, 1943), 39–40.

28. J. Edwin Orr, *The Event of the Century: The 1857–1858 Awakening,* ed. by Richard Owen Roberts (Wheaton: International Awakening Press, 1989), 19–22. Orr carefully points out that the revival cannot be explained in terms of the bank panic. The prayer meetings had begun before the economic crisis and continued long after the crisis had passed.

29. See John D. Hannah, "The Layman's Prayer Revival of 1858," *Bibliotheca Sacra* 134 (January-March 1977) : 59–73.

30. Even Charles Finney acknowledges that the revival put him and other ministers in the shadows (see *Memoirs*, 562).

31. Rudolph, *The American College and University,* 83 and Orr, *The Event of the Century,* 178ff.

32. Orr, *The Event of the Century,* 178, referencing the *Oberlin Evangelist,* 28 April 1858.

33. Tyler, *History of Amherst College During its First Half Century 1821–1871,* 454–55. Stearns went on to say, "How they will hold out, time must show. Generally in such cases, some fall back. But many circumstances inspire us with unusual confidence that this unhappy number will be small." See Tyler, 455.

34. Rudolph, *The American College and University,* 84.

35. Orr, *Campus Aflame,* 79.

36. See *Glory Filled the Land: A Trilogy on the Welsh Revival (1904–1905),* ed. by Richard Owen Roberts (Wheaton: International Awakening Press, 1989).

37. See Richard M. Riss, *A Survey of 20th-Century Revival Movements in North America* (Peabody, Mass.: Hendrickson Publishers, Inc., 1988) for helpful material on Azusa Street. Earle Cairns argues that the Azusa Street Revival should have greater priority since it eventually launched a worldwide movement. See Cairns, *An Endless Line of Splendor,* 177.

38. See Orr, *Campus Aflame*, 115–22.

39. *Intercollegian*, Chicago, Vol. 27, April 1905, 167, cited in Orr, *Campus Aflame*, 115.

40. C. Hoyt Watson, manuscript, *History of Seattle Pacific College*, 20, cited in Orr, *Campus Aflame*, 120.

41. Duewel, *Revival Fire*, 213. See also Orr, *Campus Aflame*, 131.

42. Orr, *Campus Aflame*, 130.

43. Hoffman, *Revival Times in America*, 164.

44. *The Standard*, Chicago, May 6 & 13, 1949, cited in Orr, *Campus Aflame*, 171.

45. Hoffman, *Revival Times in America*, 164 and J. Edwin Orr, *Good News in Bad Times: Signs of Revival* (Grand Rapids: Zondervan, 1953), 54–85. Orr also notes there were other schools which attempted to "organize" revival but "failed pathetically" (81).

46. W. W. Holland, cited in Henry C. James, *God's People Revived: An Account of the Spontaneous Revival at Asbury College in February 1950* (Wilmore, Kentucky: Asbury Theological Seminary, 1957), 7–8. Henry James was a resident of Wilmore who was converted during the revival. For his testimony, see pages 62–63.

47. McKenna, *The Coming Great Awakening*, 19. Among the noteworthy names that should be added to the list is Richard Halverson, for many years chaplain of the United States Senate. See Orr, *Campus Aflame*, 173 for an account of how Halverson was impacted during this period.

In light of the way God has honored the ministry of these and others touched by revival during this period, J. Edwin Orr's words written in 1953 seem prophetic: "It appeared as if the Holy Spirit had begun to raise up a new generation of revived leaders, who, when they reach places of responsibility in their respective denominations, will lend their influence to the support of a program of revival and cooperative evangelism." See Orr, *Good News in Bad Times*, 85.

48. This has been well documented in Coleman, *One Divine Moment*.

49. Ibid., 13–14.

50. Ibid., 17–19.

51. Jeff Blake, quoted in Coleman, *One Divine Moment*, 27.

52. Robert E. Coleman, *The Spark That Ignites* (Minneapolis: World Wide Publications, 1989), 27. Coleman notes, "The lights in the building were not turned out for four months."

A revised and updated version of this book has been released under the title *The Coming World Revival* (Wheaton: Crossway, 1995).

53. Coleman, *The Spark That Ignites*, 26.

54. Coleman, *One Divine Moment*, 55.

55. Tom Carruth, "Special Report No. 4," Department of Prayer and Spiritual Life, Asbury Theological Seminary, February 11, 1970. *Chris-*

tianity Today also ran an article describing the impact of the Asbury revival on other campuses. See John Nelson and Janet Rohler, "Asbury Revival Blazes Cross-Country Trail," *Christianity Today,* March 13, 1970, 46–50.

For a detailed account of how the 1970 Revival impacted Southwestern Baptist Theological Seminary, see Timothy K. Beougher, "Times of Refreshing: The Revival of 1970 at Southwestern Baptist Theological Seminary," in *Evangelism for a Changing World,* ed. by Timothy K. Beougher and Alvin L. Reid (Wheaton: Harold Shaw Publishers, 1995), 215–31.

56. Gary Stratton, "The Renewal Movement at Gordon College," April 1995 (typewritten), 1.

57. Douglas Hyde, *Dedication and Leadership* (Notre Dame, Ind.: Univ. of Notre Dame Press, 1966), 17. I am grateful to Rev. Thomas Bassford for calling this quote to my attention.

58. McKenna, *The Coming Great Awakening,* 59.

3
Wheaton's Past Revivals

Mary Dorsett

Mary Dorsett has a master of arts degree from Wheaton Graduate School. Material in this chapter was originally published as an article for Wheaton Alumni *(vol. 56, no. 2, April/May 1989). In the fall of 1994, it was expanded and published as a pamphlet by International Awakening Press, Wheaton, Illinois.*

"If my people, who are called by my name, will humble themselves and pray and seek my face and turn from their wicked ways, then will I hear from heaven and will forgive their sin and will heal their land" (2 Chron. 7:14). For years the college selected this verse to set the tone for the day of prayer which preceded each week of special or evangelistic services on campus. Believing the promises for forgiveness and healing to be real, members of the community gathered to ask God for revival. Some prayer groups met for twenty-four or more hours as they beseeched the Holy Spirit to challenge, refresh, and renew the vision of the college.

Struggle marked the early history of Wheaton College. Founded at the start of the Civil War, the small college clung tenaciously to life as it faced the problems of wartime shortages, most notably of funding and students. Prospective faculty understood that the meager salary promised would not be enough to sustain a family, and in the early years, the professors augmented their income in creative ways that included farming, pastoring, or the boarding of students. In his autobiography, Charles Blanchard, the president of Wheaton College from 1882–1925, explained that the school paid all debts in full at the end of each month, and then the remainder of available cash was divided "pro rata among the teachers. . . . Whenever a new teacher was about to be taken onto the staff, he was first made fully acquainted with this method for carrying on. He was free to accept or reject the offer. If he did not want to be one with such a self-sacrificing band of workers he was not taken on."[1]

Yet the power of the Holy Spirit flourished in the midst of this financial poverty. From its earliest days, the college experienced strong and repeated visitations of the Spirit. In these early years, new students were not required to be professing Christians, and the fruit from revivals often manifested itself by spiritually awakening the hearts of these young people. *The Christian Cynosure,* the newspaper founded by Jonathan Blanchard and others in 1868, carried frequent accounts of students being saved. Between 1878 and 1895, there were at least ten different reports of revival. Weekly student prayer meetings, special days for prayer and fasting, and the need for specific times of confession and the seeking of God's face were born from this rich spiritual heritage.

By the 1930s it was college tradition to use the verse from 2 Chronicles to set the tone for the day of prayer which preceded each week of "special" or "evangelistic" services on campus. In 1943 Julia Blanchard, daughter of Charles Blanchard, told the *Record* that these special services came about as a result of a serious illness experienced by her father. "Dr. Blanchard felt . . . that something should be done for the spiritual benefit of the students; therefore regular weeks at the beginning of each semester were set aside for evangelistic meetings.[2]

Believing the promises of forgiveness and healing to be real, members of the community gathered to ask God for revival. Some prayer groups met for twenty-four or more hours as they beseeched the Holy Spirit to challenge, refresh, and renew the vision of the college. Occasionally the answer took a dramatic form.

1936

During the fall semester of 1935, a Wheaton gospel team visited Toronto and met Irish evangelist J. Edwin Orr. As a result of this encounter, some of the team members—including Jack Murray and Don Hillis (a campus leader and pastor of the local Gospel Tabernacle church), Adrian Heaton, and Robert Evans—felt led to pray for revival on campus. When they returned to the college, they began earnestly praying for their community. In January 1936, when Orr came to speak in chapel, Don Hillis sought him out to tell him about the prayer group and to ask when they should expect revival to come to campus. Orr replied, "Whenever Christians get right with God about their sins."[3]

Less than a month later, Dr. Robert C. McQuilkin set the tone for the 1936 mid-winter evangelistic services with the challenge: "This is the week for taking the most important major that you will ever have in college, a major in knowing Christ and making him known."[4] These services with Dr. McQuilkin, president of Columbia Bible College and a popular campus speaker, were eagerly anticipated by the students. Even though Dr. McQuilkin had spoken in 1935, he had been invited to return because his messages had been so favorably received by the students.[5] McQuilkin's earlier services, which focused on living the victorious life, were remembered as a "time of renewed consecration and spiritual zeal." In preparation for the 1936 meetings, the students had poured out their hearts in prayer, anticipating the blessings of Dr. McQuilkin's series.[6]

Dr. McQuilkin spoke, as scheduled, on Sunday and Monday nights, but fell ill with influenza on Tuesday and spent the remainder of the week in bed. Guest speakers filled the pulpit while Homer Hammontree and Bill Thomas led the singing.[7]

On Thursday morning, February 6, Dr. Walter L. Wilson, a Kansas City radio evangelist, spoke to the students. At the end of his message Dr. Wallace Emerson, the dean of men, "rose to say that he could not understand what was hindering the work of the Spirit—perhaps there was unconfessed sin."[8]

The next person on his feet was senior Don Hillis, lamenting the fact that Wheaton students so feared emotion that they often hindered the work of the Spirit. Hillis then inquired how God-fearing Christian students could receive the fullness of the Spirit's power.[9] Greatly respected by the student body, Don electrified the congregation when he then proceeded to publicly confess sin in his life. Soon another student rose and asked forgiveness.

Before long it became apparent to the congregation that the Holy Spirit was present in a very special way. Confession followed confession; classes were canceled for the remainder of the day, and people skipped lunch. Following a brief pause for dinner, the chapel filled for the evening service. At 7:00 P.M. confessions and testimonies resumed, lasting until the wee hours of the morning.

Bob Hess had transferred to Wheaton in the fall of 1935 and found a job working in the kitchen. He was scheduled to assist the cook with lunch and consequently left the chapel soon after the revival began. On the way to work, he remembers meeting another student who had skipped chapel and was glad to see Bob, as the student "thought the rapture might have taken place, and he was left." Assured by Bob that chapel was extended, the relieved student "hurried to his absent seat and in time made his peace with God."[10]

Many people on campus viewed the day's events as the answer to fervent prayer. During the week preceding the revival, the *Record* ran an editorial reminding the student body of the challenge and outcome of Dr. McQuilkin's message the previous year.[11] Those who responded to the call for complete consecration had been "lifted to a new plane of spiritual growth," but there remained a portion of the campus who "refused to answer the Master's call."

Those who sincerely and deeply desired the outpouring of the Holy Spirit had been meeting regularly to pray for the college and everyone associated with it; students had been humbly praying for revival for as long as two years before the Holy Spirit poured out His blessing. The *Record* quotes President Buswell as saying, "It was a rebuke to our faith that those we counted on most to bring revival blessings were all laid aside, so that when we might least expect it, the Lord sent us such great blessings."[12]

Powerful changes resulted on campus, according to senior Bob Walter, as "the old, familiar hardness of spirit [was] replaced by a tender humility. Many, many apologies were exchanged; many restitutions made. This went on for days. It was a different campus. Even members of the faculty made apologies."[13]

In the weeks that followed, attendance at student prayer meetings rose dramatically, as did the number of volunteers for Christian service projects and activities.[14] The long-term effects of the 1936 Revival can still be felt today, as many student participants went on to dedicate their lives to the ministry of God. Several Wheaton students, including Will Norton, Neill Hawkins, Peter Stam III, and Herbert Anderson, were involved in the founding and early years of the Student Foreign Missions Fellowship, as each took a turn as the acting general secretary before going to the mission field themselves. Many dedicated career missionaries, including numerous Wheaton graduates, were raised up from the SFMF. The eventual merger of SFMF with the missions wing of InterVarsity Christian Fellowship contributed to the birth of the Urbana Missionary Conventions.[15]

The classes of 1934–37 produced a higher percentage of full-time Christian workers than any other period in Wheaton's history: 1934–38 percent; 1935–36 percent; 1936–33 percent;

1937–31 percent.[16] These figures are significantly higher than those in the preceding or following years.

1943

In 1943 Dr. Edman called for a special day of prayer to precede the mid-winter evangelistic services. "Concentrating on this week's evangelistic emphasis, the entire college family suspended the regular class schedule today [Tuesday, February 9] to spend time in prayer. This day of prayer has been called at irregular intervals by President Edman as the campus need presented itself."[17]

Prior to this time, students had been meeting in small groups all over the campus in preparation for the services. Larry Ward remembered:

> It was during the last week of January, 1943—my last night on campus before entering what was to become a three-year period of military service. I was packed and ready to go, but something had drawn me from my room in Glen Ellyn to walk the campus one last time—and to stop for a moment of reflection in the chapel. . . . I can't recall what led me to go upstairs in the chapel—or what caused me to pause outside one door and listen to the quiet murmurs from inside.
>
> But I do remember, most vividly, what I saw when I dared to open the door. Here were five or six students on their knees, praying—praying, I quickly sensed, for revival on Wheaton's campus. No campus leaders, these. No BMOC whom I could recognize. There was nothing holier-than-thou—nothing judgmental. But I can still feel the incredible warmth of that room, the special something which drew me inside. One of the fellows (whom I recognized from having worked with him briefly, washing dishes in the college kitchen) had apparently sensed my

presence. He looked up and motioned me to join them, but I was already beginning to kneel.

I remember walking back home later, still feeling the glow of that very special time—and I suppose my reaction was basically pretty selfish. I was thinking how special this unexpected experience had been for *me*—what a beautiful benediction it had been to my short semester plus at Wheaton before heading off to the unknown challenges of army life.

But a few weeks later, somewhere across the USA with Uncle Sam, I picked up a Christian periodical. . . . It was just a short news item, but the heading jumped out at me from the page . . . "Revival at Wheaton."

And as I read it, I felt again the warmth of that little upper room—saw those concerned faces, heard the sweet earnestness of their prayer—and sensed how now they must be rejoicing that God had heard from heaven and healed their campus.[18]

This time the speaker, the Reverend Harold P. Warren, was a relatively unknown pastor from Flint, Michigan. For the Sunday afternoon session, a "union" meeting with area churches, Pastor Warren chose the familiar passage from 2 Chronicles 7:14 as his text.[19]

On Tuesday, February 9, the *Record* printed a brief biographical sketch of Pastor Warren, which noted his journey from atheism to Spirit-filled minister. A letter from Pastor Warren in the college archives relates that he arrived on campus "frightened to death!" This was the first week-long service that he had conducted outside of his own church. He was scheduled to speak morning and evening each day of that week.

I felt burdened by the Lord to preach on *sin*. I will always remember that on Thurs. morning in the chapel, after my message, I gave the invitation for students to get right with God. At that moment a young man, a prominent athlete, came running down the center aisle and up on the platform and asked if he might say what was on his heart to the students.[20]

The student, Duncan Stewart, captain of the cross-country team, confessed "with penitent spirit and voice" to violating the Sabbath by leading some members of the team in a meet on Sunday without the knowledge of the school. He further admitted having "taken another student's notes without his permission in order to study for an exam."[21] As Pastor Warren recalled, "The students all knew him well and respected him and thus were all broken up themselves. Before he was through talking, MANY of the students were standing at their own seats, greatly moved and weeping, and were waiting to confess their own sins and ask forgiveness."[22]

In a pattern similar to that of the Revival of 1936, the confessions continued throughout the day as students skipped lunch, dinner, and classes. Harry Shaffer wrote to his parents that Pastor Warren

is not an emotional speaker such as we usually have here, but is quiet, very frank and humble at the same time. . . . He spoke of the lack of inward searching and of the prominence of considering other people's sins rather than our own. Psalm 139 was placed before us, verses 23 and 24 in particular. "Search *me*, O God, and know *my* heart: try *me* and know *my* thoughts: and see if there be any wicked way in *me*, and lead me in the way everlasting." Several people raised their hands and went forward to accept Christ as their Savior from their sins, on Wednesday night. We thought that was quite wonderful, but it was nothing as compared to what happened yesterday. [After relating the start of the revival, he went on to recall its effect on him personally.] . . . Everyone who works in the dining hall takes it for granted that he or she can eat anything he wants, regardless of the payment for it . . . that was a "worker's privilege." But every worker saw yesterday that he had done wrong. Sister never took extra items until she saw me do it. I was a *stumbling block* to her. I knew that last week and that I should stop, but I didn't, and it seemed as though I couldn't even pray nor even want any to be saved in these meetings, because that was a *sin* in my life. I just hoped the meeting would end so I would not have to confess that I had done anything like that. I never saw pride work any harder than it did in me, and when the president finally said the meeting would close after those standing were through talking, I was a bit relieved, but I felt so guilty. Mommy, I finally stood up before every one was through and after standing nearly an hour, I was finally called upon and said what I had done. Sister came over and sat beside me, she had stood, too. When I realized I was hungry, I thought it must be about 12:00 noon. Sister said it was ten of four.[23]

The testimonies were briefly suspended Thursday evening as Pastor Warren presented his message. However, they quickly resumed at the conclusion of the service and continued until midnight, when President Edman stopped them so that students could get some rest.

Friday morning began as usual, but this time Pastor Warren concluded his morning message with

something I never thought I could do—I turned to the faculty that was seated on the platform back of me and said something like this: "I rejoice to see what is taking place among these students, BUT I wonder if there is a similar spiritual need among the faculty?" It seemed the Holy Spirit came down upon that group of men and women and broke THEM up—one after another they stood, greatly moved with tears and broken voice, they acknowledged THEIR own need for forgiveness and a closer walk with the Lord.[24]

The testimonies and confessions again proceeded unhindered until midnight, and the closing meeting on Sunday afternoon turned into an unforgettable praise service.

The campus had been touched in a special way. It was Dr. Edman's opinion that every "student, faculty member and staff of the college has been touched by the Holy Spirit in this Revival."[25] As had happened in 1936, the campus felt the effects of the cleansing and renewing. A rekindled devotion to prayer and the discipline of the Spirit-filled life remained apparent for quite some time.[26] More than 30 percent of the class of '43 ultimately became involved in some form of full-time Christian ministry either at home or overseas.[27]

The spiritual sensitivity on campus was further bolstered as veterans returning from World War II brought a touch of maturity not always found in the student body. The spiritual effects of the two revivals remained on campus long after the actual events ended, and the classes from the late 1940s continued to produce an enormous number of full-time Christian workers scattered in many parts of the world.

1950

The fall of 1949 began as usual, but some astute members of the college noticed an increased seriousness about spiritual matters on the part of the students. At the senior retreat, prayer requests centered on spiritual needs for family and friends who did not know the Lord as friend and Savior. One person attending, Phyllis Brattland, an only child, a talented soloist and very popular member of the senior class, requested prayer for her parents. Just a few weeks later, the student body was stunned when they learned that Phyllis had been killed in an automobile accident on an icy road. The campus had observed her life of vibrant faith and constant readiness to meet the Lord; now her death called many to question their own future in the light of eternal values.[28]

The week before the winter evangelistic services were scheduled to begin, Dr. Torrey Johnson, who had graduated from Wheaton in 1930 and was founder of Youth for Christ, conducted a similar series at Wheaton Academy. On Monday, January 30, Mrs. Edman organized a prayer meeting for mothers of the academy students, and the Holy Spirit answered their prayers in a very direct way. Each mother felt burdened to seek out her child. The mothers then proceeded to make a confession of their own sin to the surprised youth. The service that evening was exceptionally powerful, and by Wednesday every student in the Academy had become a disciple of Jesus. The Academy then began praying for the college.[29]

For the opening college session on Sunday night, February 4, 1950, Dr. Edwin Johnson used 2 Chronicles 20:12: "O our God, will you not judge them? For we have no power to face this vast army that is attacking us. We do not know what to do, but our eyes are upon you." Stressing that sin clogs lives, he urged his hearers to clean their lives of all that blocked God's power. Only a few of the many students who filled the alumni gym responded to the invitation, but this was the standard reaction to such services, and the campus remained unaware of the coming revival.[30]

Monday's services appeared normal in all respects, and a day of prayer was announced for the following day. In the Tuesday afternoon prayer and praise session, a time was allotted for testimonies. One of the speakers, Dr. Clarence Hale, professor of Greek and a truly humble and respected man on campus, came forward. Dr. Hale came to the microphone to confess publicly that he was guilty of speaking unkindly to students about another member of the faculty; he then asked to be forgiven. The student body immediately came to life. This was something they had not seen before, and several students followed Dr. Hale's example and openly confessed sin, but the power of the Holy Spirit remained hidden from the congregation.[31]

Wednesday proceeded in a normal fashion until the evening meeting, when Dr. Edman asked for a few testimonies following the singing of the chorus that began "Send a great revival in my soul." Earlier that day, senior Bill Kornfield had requested Dr. Edman's permission to speak at the evening service. He was the first one on his feet when the call came, but others quickly followed his lead. Dr. Edman had mentally set aside ten minutes for the testimonies. When Eugene Lye stood, the president acknowledged him but indicated that he would be last. Before Gene could finish speaking, several others waited to take his place, and this pattern continued all night.[32]

As with the other revivals, the testimonies and confessions followed a Spirit-ordained order. Most were very brief, lasting only a few minutes, and although specific in the naming of sins such as cheating, pledge breaking, pride, bitterness, resentment etc., they avoided the sensational. This time President Edman did not dismiss the meeting but let it run all Wednesday night. At first fifty to one hundred students stood for hours, waiting their turn at the microphone. Finally someone suggested that they sit in the faculty or choir seats behind the podium while waiting to testify. From top to bottom, those waiting moved in snakelike fashion while they prayerfully anticipated speaking. In addition to the main meeting, faculty and staff also counseled and prayed with students in smaller rooms in Pierce Chapel.

Spontaneous prayer and praise gatherings sprung up in many dormitories and houses as newly forgiven students attested to the Spirit's transforming power. Excerpts from a letter written by student Roy Wilbee to his future wife, Betty, recount events with his roommates very early Friday morning.

> Last night I came home about 1:30 and was going to bed, but I just sat fascinated listening to [another student], who was saved

Thursday morning. He just sat there and it just kept bubbling out. He was one of the group of fellows on the campus who have just been living terrible lives. . . . They have been breaking everything in the pledge (except secret societies), stealing from the Stupe and putting slugs in the college phones. Last night [he] was digging out a lot of athletic equipment out of his closet that he had swiped last year. He figured he owed the Stupe about $50 and he was fired from working in the Stupe a couple of months ago because they knew he was taking meal tickets. He would get them charged up to himself, and then go and tear up the charge sheet. I could go on telling you more that kids have done, but their attitudes now are so much more wonderful to talk about. [He] just went on last night telling how wonderful it all was. He said "Boy, when you fellows had that prayer meeting in the house here, and Earl was about in tears, and Al said how wonderful it was, I thought, 'How stupid, it's absolutely ridiculous.' You guys name the night for a meeting, and I'll be sure to go out."[33]

The debate team was in a motel room in Florida on Wednesday evening and was totally unaware of events on campus. Senior Bill Thompson "was engaged in his devotions, when suddenly he became overwhelmed with heart searching—knew himself to be critical, hateful, saying things he shouldn't, conceited. He had to go at once and admit his faults to other team members. This brought the whole debate team to their knees before God and making things right with each other. This was the pattern the awakening was taking in Pierce Chapel, one thousand miles away, at that very same moment. What more convincing sign could come from the hand of God?" The Chapel Choir, on tour in the south, had a similar experience, thus bringing revival to even the far-flung members of the community.[34]

Foreign and domestic newspapers quickly picked up the story, and Thursday's headlines blazed, "Students and Teachers Quit Classes in Non-Stop Prayer Meeting," "Revival Meeting

Reaches High Pitch," "1,500 STUDENTS PRAY ALL NIGHT, KEEP ON: Fervor Grips Wheaton Hall." The student body rose for an early breakfast on Thursday morning before returning to chapel, where they discovered almost a hundred classmates still waiting to address the group.[35] Dr. Edman later prepared an account of these days.

> Some have wondered how we could be so long, thirty-nine successive hours in chapel—Wednesday night, all day Thursday, Thursday night, until Friday morning; and then we continued the service in one of the smaller rooms of the chapel. If you had been with us, you would have felt the presence and power of God. A newspaper man from Chicago who came to us, in his own words, "with the cynicism of his trade," remained to marvel at the earnestness and sincerity of the students. When one had met the Lord Jesus in reality, it did not seem long to wait six or eight hours to give one's testimony. Some saved and unsurrendered students sat for more than twenty-four hours in chapel before their hearts were broken and melted by the Spirit of God. A student from the University of Chicago heard a radio announcement of what was transpiring at Wheaton, and drove out to see what was happening. He sat in chapel from ten in the evening until three in the morning and then sought someone to help him find the Saviour. A high school student, passing the chapel at eleven o'clock, felt drawn in, and was led to the Saviour.[36]

Thelma Pugh Krohn, a sophomore at the time of the revival, typified many students. Her notes from the time record her initial skepticism:

> I confess my stubborn and proud spirit didn't really enter into the spirit of the testimonies for a long while. I had not done some of the things that others said they had done. Wasn't I pretty good?

> Slowly I knew the Lord was speaking to me about things I ought to make right. I knew He wanted me to go to the platform, too, but I argued with Him and didn't want to give in.
>
> Many things began to come over me. I knew I had a horrible attitude during freshman initiation last year and had probably caused many to stumble. I knew I had criticized people. However, I wasn't quite willing to get up there in front of all those people and make things right.

Thelma and her roommate, Ann, listened all night before leaving the chapel at noon on Thursday to get something to eat. While walking across campus, it occurred to her that she had neglected all of her regular activities for the last seventeen hours—no studying, sleep, trips to the Campus Post Office, or writing in her diary, but now nothing mattered except "the finding of God's will for our lives and knowing His perfect peace. . . ." Returning to chapel after lunch, she surrendered to the Spirit and told Ann that she was going to the platform. Little did she expect an eight-hour wait, but the Lord used the time before she spoke to help her understand how her "pride and willfulness" kept her from being fully devoted to him. Pierce Chapel filled to overflowing on Thursday evening before she spoke at 9:00 P.M. "It was very humiliating to get up there in front of all those people and say the things I knew I had to say, but it had to be done."[37]

Midnight came, but the number waiting to speak did not diminish, and the testimonies continued through the night until 9:00 Friday morning, when Dr. Edman officially halted them. Those still wishing to speak were instructed to go to one of the prayer rooms, where they could continue the meeting. As more and more outsiders were arriving, the president feared that the press and others might misinterpret or sensationalize the events. The speaker, "Pastor Ed," spoke at the chapel hour on Friday morning, and classes were resumed at noon. Most of the campus badly needed rest.

Friday evening, Pierce filled to capacity, and more than one participant commented that the singing of "Wonderful Grace of Jesus" presented a glimpse of heavenly praise. Following the service, Knight and Arrow Halls once again filled as students and townspeople brought friends from the area to hear more about Jesus. A spontaneous "Singspiration" broke out after the official service and continued until the early hours of Saturday morning. The pattern repeated itself for Saturday morning's voluntary chapel, as many stood for the crowded service in Pierce.[38]

Monday, February 13, brought a terrible snow and ice storm. As a result, the campus was without electricity, and a final meeting had been planned for that evening. Pastor Ed had not returned to Seattle as originally planned so that he could take part. With the help of generators provided by the Physics Department, enough energy was supplied to run eight main lights, the public address system, and the lobby lights in the Alumni Gym. Students with flashlights came to the cold building, sat in the dark, prayed, listened to Pastor Ed, and sang praises to the Lord with renewed conviction. According to one account, "More than 2,300 people packed into the building to hear Dr. Johnson. An overflow crowd of 300 listened in Pierce chapel.[39] By all accounts, it was a glorious service.[40]

In a letter dated March 5, 1950 from Philip B. Marquart, M.D., a psychiatrist and professor of psychology at Wheaton from 1945–58, to Dr. David Howard, who had graduated from Wheaton the previous year, Dr. Marquart wrote of the power of the Holy Spirit and the order of revival.

> Like all true revival, as Edwin Orr told us last year, this one began with the most consecrated saints seeking forgiveness, then followed the less consecrated, and finally in the early morning hours of Thursday those pledge-breakers who were coming home from dances, dropped in to see the fun in Pierce Chapel—and when they heard public confession of sins less than their own, they

tearfully fell to their knees. Finally, the unsaved students came through, about a dozen of them—one of the Edman boys among them. Last, curious outsiders from Wheaton and Chicago came to scoff and remained to pray. One was a Chicago businessman; another was an atheist from the University of Chicago. Clifton Utley himself says over his broadcast that he'll never be the same again after seeing the Wheaton revival.

At this point, I went out to eat. Found a high school boy in Walgreens, just longing to be saved. Led him to Christ. Took him to church, where he made his public profession. Then took him home and left him trying to lead one of his high school friends to Christ. That is just an example of how the Lord had prepared hearts all over the Chicago area for His word. Even Wheaton people are hungering for it. One day [I] went down in Wheaton and had the opportunity to give a plain, matter-of-fact testimony to four businessmen who ordinarily would have scoffed and scorned.

We all found things wrong with ourselves and got right with God—when his search light showed us whether there be wicked ways in us—and there were. We all found we were just sinners saved by grace and that it was a mercy that we were not consumed. I found myself to be filled with pride, resentment, and bitterness and that I keep my tongue wagging when it should be still etc. All the jealousies and antagonisms in the faculty are now dissolved away in the love of Christ. It's wonderful to be a group where everybody loves everybody else. It is most thoroughly normal.

Now here are some of the astounding psychological facts. . . . Several dozen cases of emotional problems melted away in revival. I lost all my student counseling interviews. One by one they came around and declared that they were cured. So I merely asked them to return once more to give their testimony—which I wrote down in my revival notebook. That means that if we had continuous revival all over the world, believers would need psychiatry much less than they do. I began to wonder whether the Lord wasn't rejecting, for me, the idea of psychiatry of any kind. Then I began to get an avalanche of new patients. Most of them were under conviction—and in conviction it is possible to get every kind of mental abnormality, as long as they resist. One student who had scoffed at the revival became beset with a serious phobia—a fear that he might be catching epilepsy. This phobia was the punishment for his scoffing. Secular methods were of no avail. Finally I led him to confess to the Lord. Here he resisted. He had scorned the revival in the first place because he was against confession. As soon as he confessed, his phobia left him.

Yes, of course, the world can't understand, but you can be proud of your school, for revival has flowed right out from Pierce Chapel to all parts of America.[41]

The truth of this statement has been attested by the fact that 39 percent of the class of 1950 devoted at least part of their lives to full-time Christian ministry.[42]

In the same spirit, Pastor Ed penned an open letter to all Wheaton students as he returned to his home in Seattle:

Beloved Wheaton students!

Sitting on the Pullman looking out over the barren and wintry South Dakota plains, I am asking God to help me to sanely and spiritually evaluate the days I was privileged to spend with you. I am sure I shall never be the same again. If ever I had a yielded desire to be a "ditch" for God, it is now. It is later than we think, and God is laying upon my heart the urgency of NOW as never before.

I have been thinking of you at school and in your classes. It has been revival—real revival—deep, searching revival.

But revival is not the end! It is God's means to an end! Revival is simply getting the channels cleared for use, simply getting things out of the way that have hindered. It is the ongoing life in

Christ that now counts. Now the rivers of living water can flow through us to the salvation of others.

Revival cannot plant seeds of pride. Revival is humbling. That we needed God's grace so bounteously bestowed because of confessed sins and wrongs in our lives is reason for humility. God did something because it was so sorely needed. He couldn't use us. We were on the shelf.

Can He now? Will He now? That depends upon you, each and every one. A life surrendered to Him and lived to please Him will certainly be used by Him. The community must see Christ radiant and foremost in our daily lives in order to be impressed by revival. Otherwise the name of Jesus is held up to scorn and mockery through us.

Let us live so close to God that the first entrance of sin may be discerned and confessed immediately. The cleansing of the blood of Christ, the sanctifying enabling of the Spirit, and the reality of a day-by-day fellowship with God will send us forth to triumphs in the Gospel to the ends of the world. "Unto Him that is able . . . according to the power that worketh in us . . . be glory."

February 17, 1950
Edwin S. Johnson[43]

Many have gone forth from Wheaton to do just what Pastor Johnson described: surrender their lives in order for the world to see and meet Jesus. One of the long-term fruits of the 1950 revival can be seen in radio station ELWA in Liberia, Africa. Just a week after the revival ended, Bill Watkins, Merle Steely, and Ernie Howard went to seek advice from Dr. Edman about their dream to establish a missionary radio station. At his suggestion, they formed a nonprofit organization. Other students quickly joined them, and with far more faith than money, they began their work. By 1952 Bill, Merle, Dick Reed, and their wives were in Africa, and missionary station ELWA went on the air in January 1954. Before civil war rent the fabric of Liberia in the early 1990s, ELWA had five transmitters and sent the gospel in forty-two languages to Africa, Europe, the Middle East, and even Russia. This is one of the more striking outcomes of a revival, but many equally thrilling tales remain to be told.[44]

1970

The revivals of 1936, 1943, and 1950 led some to believe that revival would continue to happen every seven years at Wheaton, but this was not to be the case. Spiritual services were held regularly and without undue attention until Thursday, February 12, of winter spiritual emphasis week in 1970. Dr. Raymond Ortlund from California was the speaker for the week. On Thursday evening, a time of testimonies preceded the evening message. Just as had happened twenty years before, students came slowly at first, but the trickle produced a steady flow that continued all night. According to an editorial in the *Record,* two occurrences—an increased spiritual concern among the freshman class and revivals at other colleges in the country—gave clues that pointed toward revival, but no one on campus actually foresaw its coming.[45]

Testimonies followed the traditional pattern of being sincere, forthright, but basically unemotional. Because the evening service was not compulsory, many students first learned of the revival over WETN radio. Throughout the night, many monitored the events in Edman Chapel as two long rows of students waited for their turn at the podium and others came and went from the chapel.[46]

The reaction on campus was mixed. Some continued to scoff, but many sensed a freshness and unity that was previously missing. Hearts that had only recently been closed to peers now reached out, and sharing took place on a much deeper level. For those involved in the service, the day became a personal spiritual milestone.[47]

1995

Between 1970 and 1995 there had been times when small groups of students felt the touch of the Holy Spirit, but the college as a whole had not been the recipient of this special blessing. Although each generation must humbly seek the face of the Lord for itself, it was and is the responsibility and privilege of all who love Wheaton to pray that a continual spirit of repentance and renewal will always be a part of her heritage. No one can explain the timing of the Holy Spirit or why He chose the spring of 1995 to once again pour out blessing in such a unique way. But nearly all who took part in the services agree that their lives will never again be the same. Conservative estimates number between two and three hundred students who jammed the aisles on the last night. They came forward to kneel in prayer and dedicate their lives to full-time Christian ministry. Many others, unable to make their way forward, did the same from their pews. A faculty member, his voice choked with emotion and tears streaming down his face, prayed and committed them into God's care and service. So glorious was the singing that followed, some wondered how the church could contain all the joyous praise lifted to the throne in heaven.

Only eternity will reveal the full impact of God's hand on Wheaton College over the decades, but for all who take the great commission seriously, the task remains constant. God is seeking men and women who desire to be humbly submitted to His will that He might use them mightily to reconcile our lost world to Himself through His Son. The ultimate outcome of revival should always be "For Christ and His Kingdom."

Endnotes

1. Frances C. Blanchard, *The Life of Charles Albert Blanchard,* (New York: Revell, 1932), 79.
2. *The Wheaton College Record,* 16 February 1943.

3. W. Wyeth Willard, *Fire on the Prairie,* (Wheaton, Ill.: Van Kampen, 1950), 188. For more on the ministry of Dr. J. Edwin Orr and revival on college campuses, see *Campus Aflame* by J. Edwin Orr, edited by Richard Owen Roberts, (Wheaton, Ill.: International Awakening Press, 1994).

4. *Record,* 5 February 1936.

5. *Record,* 15 January 1936.

6. Ibid., 29 January 1936.

7. Ibid., 12 February 1936.

8. Letter from Robert Hess ('38) to the author, 2 October 1988 (Archives and Special Collections, Buswell Library, Wheaton College). Unless otherwise noted, all cited letters can be found in the Archives and Special Collections.

9. Ibid., and letter to the author from J. Robert Walter ('36), 7 September 1988.

10. Hess letter.

11. *Record,* 29 January 1936.

12. Ibid., 12 February 1936.

13. Walter letter.

14. Hess letter.

15. H. Wilbert Norton, *To Stir the Church: A Brief History of the Student Foreign Missions Fellowships 1936-1986,* published by the Student Foreign Missions Fellowships, 1986.

16. Total class number was derived from the number of names listed for each year in the back of the 1981 Alumni Directory and includes non-graduates. The total number for those involved in Christian service comes from a list of names supplied by the Alumni Association.

17. *Record,* 9 February 1943.

18. Personal reminiscences from Dr. Lawrence Ward ('49) in possession of the author.

19. *Wheaton Alumni,* Jan.–Feb. 1943.

20. Letter from Harold Warren to the author, 15 October 1988.

21. Letter from Donald Grollimund to the author, no date.

22. Warren letter.

23. Letter from Dr. Harry Shaffer ('44) to the author, no date.

24. Warren letter.

25. Ibid.

26. *Record,* 9 February 1950.

27. See Footnote 16.

28. Warren C. Hayes letter to the author, 8 October 1988.

29. Earle E. Cairns, *V. Raymond Edman: In the Presence of the King* (Grand Rapids, Mich.: Moody, 1972), 132; and William H. Leslie, "The Story of the Wheaton Awakening of 1950," unpublished manuscript housed in Buswell Archives, 9.

30. Leslie, 9.

31. Letters from Samuel Gray ('52), 13 September 1988; Warren Hayes ('50), 8 October 1988; Etta Miller ('51), 10 October 1988; and George Schultz to the author.

32. Gray letter and Cairns, *V. Raymond Edman,* 133.

33. Letter from Roy Wilbee ('51; '55) to the author, 21 September 1988.

34. Letter from Philip B. Marquart to David Howard ('49), 5 March 1950.

35. Leslie, and the scrapbook on the 1950 Revival, which is part of the Wheaton College Archives, Buswell Library.

36. Dr. V. Raymond Edman, "Revival at Wheaton," unpublished manuscript, Archives, Buswell Library.

37. Letter from Thelma Pugh Krohn ('52) and her account of the revival taken from 1950 letter to a friend.

38. Leslie, 16, and the scrapbook in the Archives.

39. *Revival on the Campus of Wheaton College*, pamphlet, prepared by *The Daily Journal,* Wheaton, Illinois, 1950.

40. Ibid.; and the letter from Samuel Gray.

41. Marquart letter.

42. See footnote 16.

43. Johnson letter.

44. Reminiscences of Merle Steely ('50; '58) in the Archives, Buswell Library; and V. Raymond Edman, *Not Somehow but Triumphantly,* (Grand Rapids, Mich.: Zondervan, 1965).

45. *Record,* 20 February 1970.

46. Marvin K. Mayers, "Revival at Wheaton," unpublished paper, Archives, Buswell Library.

47. Ibid.; *Record,* 20 February 1970; *Tower,* 1970.

4
The Wheaton Revival of 1995:
A Chronicle and Assessment

Lyle W. Dorsett

Lyle Dorsett is professor of educational ministries and evangelism at Wheaton College and Graduate School.

There is nothing unusual about Wheaton College students voluntarily gathering in large numbers to sing praise choruses and hymns to God. Indeed, almost every Sunday night during the regular academic year, several hundred men and women stream into Pierce Chapel at 7:30 P.M. After thirty to forty minutes of worship and prayer, a student-picked speaker addresses a topic of Christian concern. After the talk, World Christian Fellowship (WCF) concludes with one or two more songs and a brief benediction or prayer. Everyone likes to adjourn by 9:00 P.M.

Unusual Events and Visitors

Sunday night, March 19, 1995, began like any other WCF gathering. A crowd of eight or nine hundred men and women students, dressed in sweatshirts and blue jeans, ambled in between 7:25 and 7:40 P.M. This assembly is strictly voluntary, so few people arrive more than five minutes early. The fashion, so it seems to the handful of faculty, staff, and other visitors, is to arrive as close to 7:30 as possible—just when the student musicians are sending forth the first notes of an upbeat chorus. On this night a WCF worship team led the assembly in song as the lyrics flashed on a large screen. After a few numbers reverberated throughout the half-century old chapel, Matt Yarrington, a junior who served throughout the year as a WCF organizer, made some opening remarks that offered the first hint of something extraordinary. Two students from Howard Payne University in Brownwood, Texas—Brandi Maguire and James Hahn—were going to offer testimonies of an unusual outpouring of God's grace on their campus several weeks earlier. Brandi and James would each speak, and after they were finished two microphones—one at the front of each aisle—would be open to students who wanted to ask questions or make comments.

Brandi, an articulate senior, talked for several minutes on how God brought spiritual revival to her school. Just before she stepped down from the platform, she said some words along the lines of "I don't know what Wheaton wants or needs. I have no idea what God is going to do here, but I do pray that you all can experience the tremendous blessing we received at Howard Payne." Her sincerity and charity left even the most skeptical attentive and hushed. When Brandi sat down, an unusual stillness engulfed the chapel.

The quiet was interrupted when James stepped up to the microphone. He was more aggressive and prophetic than Brandi. Built like a wrestler or football player, he recalled some personal sins that he had felt constrained to confess to his fellow students in Texas. After he told us how his confession had brought reconciliation with God, deep inner peace, and a renewed sense of oneness with his fellow students, he prayed that Wheaton students could experience similar revival. Indeed, what James and Brandi said they were praying for was an outpouring of God's Spirit on Wheaton in the way awakenings had broken out in several Texas churches in January and February. These movements of praise, confession, and rededication spread to Howard Payne University, then to Southwestern Baptist Theological Seminary, and eventually to other schools and churches in Texas and Alabama.

The Service Continues

It was about 8:40 P.M. when the Texans finished testifying. The Wheaton students were strangely quiet. Matt Yarrington came forward to remind the assembly that the microphones were open but no one should feel pressured. No one, he maintained, was trying to orchestrate a replica of the Howard Payne experience. Soon after Matt stepped aside, a senior man went to the microphone on the south side of the chapel. He confessed sins of pride and asked his fellow students for forgiveness. Within a few minutes, several students were lining up at both the south and north microphones. Patiently taking turns, each one confessed sin and asked God and the campus for forgiveness.

After a while, a particularly courageous Wheaton coed came forward and confessed a sexual sin. As she spoke, her voice broke. Sobs and tears punctuated her confession. When she finished, dozens of women rushed up to embrace and pray for her, and a few of these coeds confessed similar sins. If the first man's confession made it safe to step up to the microphone, this confession made it safe to be completely transparent about even the most personal and humiliating failures. In brief, the false masks of perfection began to fall in astounding ways.

Student leader Matt, and Kevin Engel, assistant director of the college's Office of Christian Outreach, offered an occasional prayer from the platform. From time to time they also suggested the relocation of small prayer groups that clustered around the repentant students. Their comments were, however, brief and designed to keep the aisles open to the microphones. There was never an attempt to stir up emotions or keep the momentum flowing.

Around midnight a heavy thunderstorm dumped its fury on Wheaton, but the downpour failed to discourage anyone. As students felt the presence of the Holy Spirit more clearly, many were convicted to leave the assembly and share the news with their friends. In dorm rooms and apartments all over the campus, many of the twenty-three hundred undergraduates and three hundred graduate students heard the first reports of the reverent and tearful assembly ocurring in Pierce Chapel.

Sometime in the middle of the night, Chaplain Steve Kellough, Kevin Engel, the student coordinators of WCF, and a couple of faculty huddled to discuss the surprising chain of events. No one wanted to interfere with God's outpouring of grace, but it was late and classes as well as chapel were scheduled as usual for Monday morning. After prayer and discussion, there was a keen sense that the meeting should end at 6:00 A.M. Because scores of students were still in line for the microphones, everyone was promised the meeting would reconvene at 9:30 Monday evening.

The Confessions Continue

By 9:30 P.M. Monday, more than one thousand students had gathered at Pierce Chapel. With space for only twelve hundred people, the aged structure looked full, and there was a mixture of expectancy and skepticism in the air. After some singing and prayer, the microphones were opened as promised. This time long lines quickly formed along both sides of the chapel. Like the previous night, it was an orderly gathering. There were radiant smiles of joy, and there was an almost constant chorus of sobbing and crying. The widespread urge to seek God's forgiveness and the forgiveness of the college community was no respecter of class, race, or gender. Men and women, undergraduate and graduate, purposefully made their way to the front.

An undergraduate man, in a determined effort to truly repent and turn away from his sins, carried some CDs in a plastic bag up to the platform. He said he had realized for months that he should get rid of these particular items, but he had refused to obey the nudging of the Holy Spirit. As soon as he confessed and placed those stumbling blocks to inner peace on the stage, other students began to rise from their seats and slip out of the chapel. During the next hours, dozens of men and women returned to the chapel, went forward, and placed on the stage items that were disturbing their fellowship with God. Within a few hours, five large plastic garbage bags were filled with a range of items including books, magazines, videos, CDs, alcohol, and tobacco.

Sometime after midnight, it was apparent that God was indeed blessing Wheaton College in a special way. The scene brings to mind 2 Chronicles 7:14, when God told Solomon: "If my people, who are called by my name, will humble themselves and pray and seek my face and turn from their wicked ways, then will I hear from heaven and will forgive their sin and will heal their land." Countless Wheaton College students—scores of them by this second night—were calling out to God. They were humbling themselves before Him and His people. They were praying and seeking His face. They were turning from their sins in confession and repentance, and God was pouring out His peace and joy upon them.

Those who confessed were not alone in experiencing great joy. Hundreds who came to see what was happening were stirred by a powerful sense of God's presence. Many lost track of time and wanted nothing to stop the outflow of songs and prayers. The ecstasy notwithstanding, the chaplain and other faculty and staff representatives agreed that the meeting should end by 2:00 A.M. with the promise of a reconvening at 9:30 P.M. on Tuesday.

College Church Opens Its Doors

During the day on Tuesday, March 21, it was learned that the college's Conservatory of Music had student recital rehearsals scheduled in both Pierce Chapel and the larger facility, Edman Chapel. Rather than interfere with events that had been scheduled for the entire academic year, it was decided to seek an alternative place to assemble. Consequently, Pastor Kent Hughes of College Church was approached by the chaplain's office. Dr. Hughes graciously made his church's sanctuary (1,500 capacity) available for the remainder of the week.

College Church is conveniently located on the western edge of Wheaton's campus. Many students worship there on a regular basis, and there is a long-standing relationship between the two institutions. Therefore, it was an easy transition to begin Tuesday at 9:30 P.M. in the College Church sanctuary.

The relocation was obviously part of the Sovereign Lord's plan. More than thirteen hundred students and a few more faculty and staff turned out on Tuesday. As the evening wore on, more students and a few visitors slipped in as well. Once again the lines were long for the microphones. And again the meeting was halted at 2 or 2:30 A.M. with the promise of reassembly at 9:30 that evening.

Wednesday: Still Meeting and Still Growing

On Wednesday night, soon after 9:30, College Church was filled to its 1,500 capacity. Choruses and hymns reverberated through the attractively designed new sanctuary. Dr. Duane Litfin, the college president, and two professors, Dr. Timothy Beougher and Dr. Lyle Dorsett, each spoke for a few minutes to encourage the students and urge them to follow up their renewed commitments through regular worship, Bible study, prayer, and accountability groups. By midnight or soon after, it became evident that the confessional stage of meetings was running its course. Therefore, it was announced that we would finish the open-microphone confessions by as close to 2:00 A.M. as possible and then adjourn. It was agreed that a final meeting would open at 9:30 on Thursday night to sing praises and use the open microphones for testimonies of praise and thanksgiving.

The last confession was heard at 2:45 A.M. It was after 3:00 in the morning when the last tired but joyous prayer warriors left College Church and walked back to their dormitories, houses, and apartments.

The Final Events and Exhortations

There was a festive mood as College Church began to fill near the 9:30 hour on Thursday evening, March 23. An overflow crowd of at least 1,800 occupied the pews in both the main floor and balcony. Latecomers stood in the hallways that encircled the sanctuary, and others sat in the folding chairs that were set up in the lobby at the rear of the church.

The music team was comprised of worship leader Nate Fawcett and vocalist Meridee Simon, supported by Sarah Wilkes (piano), Bryan LeMoine (drums), Christian Punches (keyboard), and Andrew Chignell (bass guitar). They had performed splendidly and tirelessly each night and were bursting with joy for the Thursday finale. After the musicians led a cheering throng who raised hands and voices heavenward for nearly an hour and Chaplain Kellough gave a brief message on Ephesians 3, the microphones were opened for words of testimony and praise. The coed who stepped forward first said that God had put Matthew 9:37-38 on her heart all day: "The harvest is plentiful but the workers are few. Ask the Lord of the harvest, therefore, to send out workers into his harvest field." She read Jesus' words and then challenged her fellow students to thank God for His outpouring of love by committing themselves to work in the harvest fields that the Lord has prepared.

This exhortation was only the first of many echoing a similar theme. A graduate student from Indonesia, Leo Sumule, testified that he had been unable to sleep all night. Led by the Holy Spirit, he went into Blanchard Hall, where he prayed in front of the names of Wheaton graduates, listed by class year, who had gone into full-time, cross-cultural missions. As he prayed and studied the names, he counted 127 men and women from the class of 1950—the last class that had experienced a powerful, multi-day revival. Leo contrasted the class of 1950 with the most recent on the board, the class of 1993. The latter had only nine names. The class of 1950 had turned out the largest number of missionaries in Wheaton's history. Indeed, only the classes of 1977 and 1979 sent more than one hundred missionaries each, with the totals in marked decline during the next years.

Evidently Leo had stayed up all night, because he tallied the missionary statistics, typed out a list, and placed copies on the platform for students to pick up and study. With passion in his voice and tears streaming down his face, Leo noted that he was here today because American missionaries went to Indonesia years ago and led his grandfather and father into a life-changing relationship with the Lord Jesus Christ. The articulate graduate student then challenged the students to go and finish the task of world evangelism that their predecessors had begun.

In a variation on the same theme, Dr. Jeanne Blumhagen, college trustee and veteran medical missionary, urged the students to see the world through clear lenses. She likened the world's needs to a log that had to be moved. Ten people were lifting one end, and the other end had one person trying to pick it up. "Let's be honest," she said. "North America is the end of the log with ten people on it. Is there any real question about where you are needed?"

In the wake of these challenges, someone slipped a note to Matt Yarrington, asking him to offer a prayer for any students who felt called to full-time Christian service. Matt took the microphone in hand at about midnight. He asked any students who felt led to dedicate their lives to full-time Christian service and would like prayer toward this end, to walk up to the platform. Matt then passed the microphone to one of the professors and asked him to offer a dedicatory prayer. The faculty member was so overcome by the student response that his voice choked with emotion. Tears streamed down his face. An observer in the balcony estimated between two and three hundred men and women stood around the platform and in the aisles as the professor prayed and committed them into God's care and service. Students later recalled that many more tried to go forward but the aisles were so filled that there was no way to get out from the pews.

For the next forty-five minutes to an hour, historic hymns and modern songs were sung with a fervor seldom experienced at Wheaton. People who were there said they completely lost track of time and enjoyed an ecstasy unlike anything they had experienced before. Several students confessed that they had sometimes wondered if the heavenly celebrations of praise to the Lamb, as described in Revelation chapter 7, would be rather tiresome—even boring. But late Thursday night they realized such a celebration could joyously go on ad infinitum. The concluding song was "Sing a Song of Celebration." The sound and spirit were so glorious that everyone expressed certainty that one day we will sing this together again in the New Jerusalem.

Evidence of Revival

Long before revival came to Wheaton in March 1995, I had asked a member of Wheaton College's class of 1950 how she knew there had been a revival that year. "How could you miss it?" she emphatically responded. It is tempting to offer her answer to the many people who have asked me the same question about the 1995 revival. For those who were present, it was indeed impossible to miss. Even those who came to the meetings to ask questions or scoff were usually convinced that something genuine and profound was happening to people's souls.

For those who were not there, however, more than a brief answer—even more than a chronicle of events—may be useful. In any case, I offer these reflections as my personal assessment of what happened in March 1995.

Without equivocation it can be said that revival came to Wheaton College. Only time will reveal the extent of the fruit, but in the six weeks between March 19, when the Howard Payne students testified, and commencement on May 7, it is clear that the college community experienced an unusual blessing and visitation from the Holy Spirit.

The evidence of true revival was overwhelming. First of all, we saw an outworking of God's promise to Solomon that "If my people, who are called by my name, will humble themselves and pray and seek my face and turn from their wicked ways, then will I hear from heaven and will forgive their sin and will heal their land" (2 Chronicles 7:14). For five nights we saw this text lived out. A group of God's people, mostly students, humbly sought the Lord. They wept before Him, prayed, and confessed their sins against Him and others. In most cases they showed marked remorse. They sought reconciliation with God and with other people with whom they were at odds, demonstrating a genuine spirit of repentance. They also turned away from sinful and destructive behavioral patterns by getting rid of articles and symbols of their personal rebelliousness. Others confessed sins of resentment and bitterness and forgave those who had sinned against them.

In the wake of continuous confessions came a renewed hunger for the Lord Jesus Christ. People were digging into the Scriptures, quoting verses, and through testimonies and songs offering praises to Christ Jesus for what He had done. I heard testimonies of students who became Christians during this revival. Hundreds of students admitted that they had been in rebellion against God through sins of commission and omission. Scores of others confessed they were in bondage to sexual sins, substance abuse, resentment, anger, hatred, and pride. As they got right with God and others, they could scarcely contain their joy.

A spirit of reverence and praise engulfed the college. For days I saw small groups of people in prayer all over the campus—outdoors, on benches and lawns, in hallways, and in empty rooms before and after classes. An unusually reverent spirit prevailed in chapel. There also was a singular tranquillity in the dining hall almost every day during the lunch hours. Indeed, boisterousness disappeared and an ethos of patience and tenderness marked Anderson Commons. Follow-up prayer meetings and discussion sessions were organized on many residence hall floors, and some larger, campus-wide meetings were called and fairly well attended for the purpose of helping students find support as they sought to walk in new, bondage-free paths with Christ.

Besides the evidence already mentioned, in my twelve years at Wheaton College I have never had so many people request copies of Robert Murray McCheyne's Bible Calendar, an item my wife, Mary, and I always keep on hand for students who want to get serious about daily Bible reading. In short, numerous students suddenly felt inspired to begin a serious commitment to time in God's Word. Beyond this, I received a constant stream of students seeking guidance for going into cross-cultural missions and pastoral or evangelistic ministry. Dozens of others sought advice about devotional reading and purposeful prayer.

Finally, it is significant that at our local church, and I am told our experience was rather typical, there has been an increase in the number of student worshipers. There is a powerfully renewed interest in the Lord Jesus Christ—in praising, worshiping, and talking about Him. There has also been expressed desire to glorify Him through genuine love lived out in obedience and service.

Why Now?

Except for questions regarding the genuineness of this revival, the most frequently asked question I receive is, "Why did it happen at this time?" Obviously this is a mystery. God is sovereign, and He will pour out His grace at the time and place of His design. Nevertheless, there is a place for responsibility among God's people. "If my people" is a constant refrain that challenges us from both testaments of the Bible. Many of God's people have faithfully sought His face, confessed coldness and sinfulness, and implored Him to revive us again.

Ever since Mary and I arrived in Wheaton in 1983, we have been aware of—and at times participated in—small groups where there has been prayer for revival. Indeed, some Wheaton alumni whom we know have been praying for years for the convicting presence and power of the Holy Spirit to come in the way He did back in 1936, 1943, and 1950. Ever since we came, we have been aware of student groups who regularly conducted Jericho walks (some call them Joshua walks). They walk around campus and encircle dormitories and other student housing facilities, all the while asking the Lord to break down the walls of indifference to Him. I know of at least one college trustee, as well as several faculty and staff persons, who regularly do the same thing.

Added to these concerted prayer efforts have been the intercessory prayers of missionaries all over the globe who have asked the Lord to bring revival to Wheaton College. Local churches, too, have held prayer meetings for revitalization of their congregations and the college community.

Prayer is certainly an underlying cause of the 1995 revival, but it still does not explain timing. In any case, added to the prayer factor are several other immediate causes. For three semesters previous to the March revival, God sent an Australian evangelist, John Lillyman, to study at Wheaton College Graduate School. Working on an M.A. in evangelism, Lillyman finished his degree in December 1994 and returned to his homeland before Christmas. Lillyman and his wife, alumna Rebecca Rupprecht, are an unusual couple. Everyone who made their acquaintance recognized their radical commitment to following Christ whatever He called them to do. Their love for Jesus was nurtured by a contagiously dynamic prayer life. They had a remarkable spiritual impact on the student community.

John Lillyman was especially burdened for revival. He spent as much time as possible with Dr. Robert Coleman, reading his books, attending his prayer meetings, and generally absorbing all that he could on revival, evangelism, and histories of great visitations of the Holy Spirit. John was particularly inspired to pray for revival at Wheaton College. He took the lead organizing a day of prayer in the autumn of 1994, and everyone who worked with this energetic Australian felt certain revival would break forth on the campus soon. Both of the Lillymans prayed with unusual urgency for revival, and they left behind a hard core team of prayer warriors whom they had mentored along the way.

Besides the significant efforts of the Lillymans, God used other people in instrumental ways. Robert Owen Roberts, a graduate student who had been inspired to pray for revival, took it upon himself to educate the entire student body about the way the Holy Spirit had visited Wheaton College in years past. A student of church history, Roberts assumed the task of getting Mary Dorsett to revise and expand her 1989 *Wheaton Alumni* magazine article on the history of revivals at the college. Roberts then oversaw the layout, illustration, and publication of Dorsett's pamphlet, *Revival at Wheaton,* which was published by International Awakening Press and is the basis of chapter three of this book. Roberts and his wife, Caroline, prayed this project through all the stages of the publication process with the goal of getting it out before the day of prayer, November 9, 1994, spearheaded by John Lillyman with the assistance of under-graduate Ian Hernandez. The result was that the pamphlet was distributed at World Christian Fellowship before November 9. In the wake of this distribution came rather widespread student awareness of the role of prayer in the revivals of the past. Consequently, many students involved in the day of prayer were purposefully interceding for God to send His Spirit to revive us again like he had done in bygone years.

Once the new semester began in early January, revival was being discussed and talked about with a seriousness—even an expectancy—unlike anything I have seen in more than a decade. For example, graduate student and admissions office counselor Terri Miller led a class discussion and presented a lecture on the history of revival at Wheaton. Nearly sixty students had read the Dorsett pamphlet before Miller spoke. They discussed what factors had been present when revival came in 1936, 1943, and 1950, and then they contrasted and compared campus conditions of 1995 with those of previous revival years. In the wake of Miller's teaching, the students agreed to pray for two weeks about what they could do to encourage or nurture an environment that would once more be conducive to spiritual renewal.

One of the factors that the students noted was that we receive fewer if any direct appeals from chapel speakers for us to confess our sins and repent of our hardness of heart—especially as these relate to our refusal to answer God's call for full-time, cross-cultural missionaries.

A few days after this observation, a chapel speaker did precisely what the students said was lacking. On February 27, Dr. James Plueddemann gave a stirring address in Edman Chapel. A former professor in the Wheaton College Christian Education Department, Plueddemann had left the college a year and a half earlier to become Director of the Society for International Missions (SIM). With humor and charity, yet with a keen sense of urgency, Plueddemann presented ten reasons why all students should seriously consider becoming missionaries.

I happened to be on the chapel platform that Monday morning. Scanning the audience of more than twenty-two hundred undergraduates, I could see that they were attentive. Although there were no signs of emotionalism, there was an unusual spirit of reflection. I thanked Plueddemann for a splendid message, and then went on my way without much further thought on the morning.

That night my Evangelism and Renewal class, which meets from seven to ten in the evening, began as usual. Less than thirty minutes before class was scheduled to end, someone raised a point about Dr. Plueddemann's chapel talk. When this person mentioned being convicted during chapel of her own sinfulness in refusing to respond to God's call, I saw two coeds in the back of the class with tears in their eyes. Two more students agreed with the student who confessed, and then a young man near the front began to cry. With some difficulty he spoke, begging everyone to forgive him for weeping. He then began to cry uncontrollably. Between convulsive sobs he said, "Oh, please forgive me for doing this. I'm not this kind of person."

This senior man was certainly not one who typically displayed his emotions. Always reasonable, serene, and undemonstrative, this behavior was, for him, truly extraordinary. It became apparent that this man, like several others, was under conviction for being closed to a nudging from God. Because his crying was so loud, I put my arm around him. As I offered comfort it was evident that class could not go on as usual. I glanced at the clock. It was 9:40 P.M. I told the class that I was going to stay on and pray with this man and with anyone else who felt led to pray. I urged all others to quietly slip out. Class was dismissed. Out of fifty to sixty people, more than thirty stayed for prayer. Many men and women confessed sins, some wept, and others offered support to their friends. At 11:00 P.M. I led in singing "Holy, Holy, Holy," and then closed the meeting with prayer.

To put it mildly, February 27 was not an ordinary Monday night class. Although something similar had happened one night two years earlier, the intensity was not as great, and fewer students had confessed sins and wept. I went home on February 27 with a keen sense that the Holy Spirit had been with us in a profound yet gentle way.

In retrospect I can see that this evening was only one signpost among several that full-scale revival was imminent. At least two student groups who had been on retreats during the weeks preceding March 19 were touched by similar precious hours of confession, tears, prayer, and praise. Likewise during the spring break in early March, the team of students and staff who went with Don Smarto's Prison Ministry outreach to Florida experienced similar blessing. Finally, on Saturday night, March 18, the Asian-American student group, Koinonia Fellowship, held a prayer and praise meeting and invited everyone on campus to come. The meeting was unusually well attended, and once again there was an awesome sense of God's presence that led to confession, prayer, praise, and joy.

Within twenty-four hours, hundreds of Wheaton students would enjoy a spiritual feast that these others had foretasted in the days and weeks before. Those of us who were part of the revival could only be grateful and pray that the flame would spread to many places.

In the wake of the revival, students were asked to testify at colleges, high schools, and local churches. Some were invited to speak to Christian student groups on secular college and university campuses. Chapter 7 relates examples of how God has continued to work through student testimonies all over the continent, as He worked on our campus through the testimonies of the students from Howard Payne University.

At the risk of being divisive, faithfulness to what happened between March 19 and 24 requires me to report that not everyone at Wheaton College celebrated the revival. Some people, for a variety of reasons, were dissociated from what was happening. A few people were ill, others were away from campus, and some confessed to being so consumed with pressing needs that they never attended the meetings. A small minority of people were outspokenly distressed over what was transpiring, calling it a display of emotionalism that was at best undignified. Overall, however, the campus and community were extremely supportive and grateful.

In the final analysis, we who were privileged to be involved in the March 1995 Revival know that we were given an undeserved, unearned, and unrepayable blessing. We offer thanks to God Almighty, and we implore Him to spread His mercies to the ends of the earth. The Revival of 1995, we pray, is not an end but a prelude to lives of holiness, love, mission, and service.

5
Filled with the Fullness of God

Stephen B. Kellough

*Stephen Kellough is the chaplain of Wheaton College. This
chapter contains the message he gave on Thursday
evening, during the final meeting of the 1995 revival at
Wheaton. This message places the revival and its follow-up
in the context of Ephesians 3.*

All of you who are here this evening are quite aware that
something special has been happening on the campus of Wheaton College in these days. As I listen to your worship and look
into your faces, I can tell that you not only know what is
happening, but you are thankful for what is happening, and you
are grateful to our Lord for the incredible outpouring of His love
that we have experienced.

Throughout the history of Wheaton College, God has chosen
to be present and active in this place. There have been special
times of spiritual awakening, and there is no doubt that we are
in the midst of one of those just now. We have received a special
visitation of God.

It would be wrong to say that it all began at 7:30 P.M. on Sunday, March 19, in Pierce Chapel at the weekly meeting of the World Christian Fellowship. There has been a significant stirring of the Spirit in the lives of individuals and in groups on campus over the last couple of weeks, throughout this semester, and well before that.

But something very unique and important happened last Sunday evening and has continued throughout this week. I'm not sure what the best terminology is to describe the events of these days. We might call it a time of "spiritual awakening" or "spiritual refreshing." Many would call it "revival"—and if revival means "coming back to life," I suppose that is a good term to use.

But let's not get stuck on terminology. Very clearly, God has been at work in the hearts of His people on our campus. We have been so pleased to welcome a special visitation of God.

Throughout the week we have cried together and we have laughed together. We have been saddened by our sinfulness, and we have rejoiced in the forgiveness that Christ can bring. We have shed tears of grief because of all of the junk in our lives. We have cried over our pride, our hatred, our lust, our sexual immorality, our cheating, our dishonesty, our materialism, our addictions, and our self-destructive behavior. The public confession of sin has been properly focused on how those sins have impacted relationships in the body of Christ here at Wheaton College.

The outpouring of our confessions has been greeted by the outpouring of God's love that has come directly from the Holy Spirit and at the same time administered through the love of the people of God. And in our clinging together in prayer, we have shed tears of joy because of the renewal that comes through sincere confession, repentance, and reconciliation.

Throughout this week I have seen healing . . . spiritual healings of the soul. People confessed their sins to God and to each other, and there was healing. It was biblical. It was Christian. It was orderly. It was sincere. And it honored our Lord.

Is all of this something that has been humanly contrived or manufactured? The evidence is otherwise. The personal sharing has been spiritually sensitive and biblically grounded. The depth and breadth of the confession, repentance, and reconciliation point to a divine initiative. Every way you look at it, we see confirmations that we are experiencing an authentic work of the Sovereign Lord who has chosen to visit us in a powerful way.

Tonight we are turning a corner. Throughout the week, our focus has been on the public confession of personal sin—something very necessary, something very biblical, and something very good. Tonight, as a body, we are deliberately moving into a mode of celebration, praise, and testimony.

And my question to you, my question to our community, is this: Where do we go from here?

There's a text of Scripture that I would like to draw to our attention this evening. It's a text that has been quoted more than once over the course of this week. It's the prayer of the apostle Paul at the close of Ephesians chapter 3, and it is a prayer that we would do well to memorize and pray in the days ahead. With the confession of sin, sincere repentance, and a commitment to purge our lives from every known sin, we are "putting off" ungodly and self-destructive behavior. The biblical challenge is to follow the putting *off* with a putting *on*. The scriptural imperative is to follow an emptying with a filling. The prayer of Ephesians 3 helps us to be filled with that which is for our good and for God's glory. Here's what it says:

> *For this reason I kneel before the Father, from whom his whole family in heaven and on earth derives its name. I pray that out of his glorious riches he may strengthen you with power through his Spirit in your inner being, so that Christ may dwell in your hearts through faith. And I pray*

that you, being rooted and established in love, may have power, together with all the saints, to grasp how wide and long and high and deep is the love of Christ, and to know this love that surpasses knowledge—that you may be filled to the measure of all the fullness of God.

Now to him who is able to do immeasurably more than all we ask or imagine, according to his power that is at work within us, to him be glory in the church and in Christ Jesus throughout all generations, for ever and ever! Amen.
Ephesians 3:14-21

What a magnificent prayer. Here's our answer to the question "What comes next?" Here's how spiritual growth takes place. It happens when we pray these petitions and when God grants to us the desires of our hearts.

There are various ways of outlining Paul's prayer in Ephesians 3. However it is outlined, it is clear that there is a singular emphasis in the petitions of this prayer, and that singular emphasis concerns a request for "spiritual power." The apostle is praying for power—for spiritual power. The apostle is calling down power from heaven—power for "the inner being," power for living, because it is in the "inner being" where life is really lived.

Now maybe all of this talk about "spiritual power" and "the inner being" sounds theoretical, impractical, or even mystical. But in reality, nothing could be more practical. Paul is seeking strength for the soul, where all decision making and choices for life are made.

The final request in the series of requests found in this prayer is the request asking "that you may be filled to the measure of all the fullness of God." This is the ultimate request of this series of petitions: "that you may be filled to the measure of all the fullness of God." God wants us to sense His real presence so completely that we might be filled up with His power, His strength, His infinite resources. When we're emptied of the junk in our lives, we need to be filled with something else. That something else, the Scripture says, should be "the fullness of God"—everything that God can provide—not just a little bit of God, but a whole lot of God. Not just a few attributes of God, but all of the attributes of God. This petition of this prayer is asking that we might be filled up with God—with His power, with His attributes, with His love—so that we can be obedient to the commands of Scripture to live like Jesus.

As fallen human beings, we will never do it perfectly on this side of heaven. But we will never do it at all without asking, and without receiving divine resources and divine strength.

Sometimes, as Christians who are frustrated by sin and confused by the pressures of the world around us, we do not know how to pray. Sometimes when we pray, we don't know if we are praying according to the will of God. In times like these, we can have confidence that we are praying properly when we pray the prayers of Scripture. Let me suggest that you consider praying this prayer of Ephesians chapter 3 in the days ahead—praying, meditating on the words, and trusting God for the answers. And now, using the words of this prayer, I want to pray for you:

> *For this reason I kneel before the Father, from whom his whole family in heaven and on earth derives its name. I pray that out of his glorious riches he may strengthen you with power through his Spirit in your inner being, so that Christ may dwell in your hearts through faith. And I pray that you, being rooted and established in love, may have power, together with all the saints, to grasp how wide and long and high and deep is the love of Christ, and to know this love that surpasses knowledge—that you may be filled to the measure of all the fullness of God.*
>
> *Now to him who is able to do immeasurably more than all we ask or imagine, according to his power that is at work within us, to him be glory in the church and in Christ Jesus throughout all generations, for ever and ever! Amen.*

And now, let me lead in prayer for our community in the days ahead. I will offer a specific request, and then I invite you to pray silently for that petition. Let us pray.

O Lord, hear the prayers of your people.

Father, we pray that the work of Your Holy Spirit would continue in our personal lives and in the corporate life of our community in the days and weeks and months ahead. . . .

Father, we pray that every member of our community would be protected from the attacks of the evil one. . . .

Father, we pray that the public reports of the events of these days will accurately reflect the dramatic work that You have done and that You are doing. . . .

Father, we pray that discussion on campus and beyond will be sensitive to issues of confidentiality. . . .

Father, we pray that efforts for follow-up and support will be appropriate to the needs of each person. . . .

And finally, Father, we give You our praise and our thanks for the incredible spiritual refreshment that we have received from You in these days. Amen.

6
Testimonies of Changed Lives

---

edited by Kevin Engel

Kevin Engel is assistant director of the Office of Christian Outreach at Wheaton College. The student testimonies here are separated by subheads, each section representing one testimony. Even though all the students whose work is printed here gave permission to use their real names, the publisher chose to protect their privacy by leaving the names out.

It was Thursday afternoon, March 2, 1995. Matt Yarrington, student chair of World Christian Fellowship (WCF), bolted into my little office on the third floor of the Memorial Student Center.

"Kev, I need to get your OK on this idea before I bring it to the cabinet meeting today," Matt said with excitement.

Matt explained that in Dr. Beougher's "History and Theology of Revival" course that day, they had discussed several faxes from a college and seminary in Texas that had experienced a revival of some sort. He asked what I thought about the possibility of inviting a few of the Texan students to speak at our Sunday night WCF meeting, a weekly missions-oriented worship service of about five hundred students.

I was wary of the idea. For years students have recounted the Wheaton revival of 1950, when classes had been canceled and students had confessed and prayed for thirty-nine hours straight. I certainly wanted to see students get right with God—that is a major part of our purpose in the Office of Christian Outreach. But I didn't want to see God's work limited to reliving a format that He had used on our campus years ago, or on some other campus weeks ago.

I told Matt how I had already seen signs of renewal all over our campus in recent years. The November 1994 all-campus day of prayer had begun at 5:30 A.M. with two hundred students crowding onto the chapel stage. And I had been hoping for twenty!

Pockets of students had organized weekly revival prayer groups every year. The discipleship small groups had grown to include seven hundred students. Racial reconciliation was happening in and through the ministry of the energetic Gospel Choir. Student-led ministries were thriving. Key faculty members were organizing for greater off-campus ministry impact. Participation in the weekly WCF meetings had more than doubled in the past three years. Maybe a different sort of spiritual awakening was already happening!

Besides, how could we possibly invite student speakers from Texas? A hundred questions whirled in my mind: Who are these students? How do I know what they will say? Are they aware of our particular campus environment? How could we decide something this important when student leaders were all leaving for spring break in twenty-four hours? And the ever-present question—who would pay for this? Our fifty-dollars-per-week budget couldn't possibly fly two students across the country at short notice.

Yet I knew from many private conversations with students that the need for a fresh cleansing of God in our lives was great.

Rather than unleashing all of my inner questioning on Matt's enthusiasm, I voiced a few mild cautions, and we prayed together for wisdom. To make a long story brief, when God moves, obstacles come down. After much prayer and conversation, we decided to move ahead. Two students from Howard Payne University, Brandi Maguire and James Hahn, came to Wheaton on March 19, 1995, to testify at the World Christian Fellowship meeting. The chain of events that followed is set forth in an earlier chapter. What is presented here are eighteen student testimonies, representative selections from hundreds, that are the crux of the story—examples of the lives that are changed when God moves. These testimonies are written as they were related by the students, each section representing one student's recollections of what happened to him or her. As you read them, you will recognize a few recurring themes:

- initial skepticism
- struggles with motivations
- gnawing conviction of sin
- doubts about public confession
- the prevalence of sexual sin
- the isolation caused by sin
- desire for reconciliation
- hunger for Scripture
- surprise at the power of prayer
- insights into God's view of sin
- steps of action for lasting change
- desire for accountability
- motivation to share with others

The students' honesty and trust in God's unconditional love humbles and inspires me. May it do the same for you.

Wrestling with Motives

This was one of the most exciting experiences I have ever had the privilege of being a part of. I have never seen God's hand on so many lives at once.

On Sunday, March 19, I had to take a friend to the airport. His flight left at 7:00 P.M., so I knew I probably would get back too late to go to WCF. I didn't arrive home until about half past nine, and they usually end around nine or a little after.

I tried to call a girl to ask her out for a date around 10:30 P.M. Her roommate was on the phone, so I said I would call back around 11:30. When I did, I was informed that she had just grabbed her coat and left. I kind of wondered what she had left for at almost midnight. A little bit later, I called over to some friends' house and was informed that no one had come home from WCF yet. This surprised me.

The next day, I went to class to find out that there had been a revival, that people had stayed at Pierce Chapel until 6:00 A.M. I was somewhat surprised and a bit curious. I heard that there had been lines of people still waiting to confess their sins at six, but that everyone was pretty tired by that time.

I started thinking cynically. People probably were just manufacturing what was going on because they wanted a revival so badly. I remember us praying for revival back during my sophomore year. I thought that people were just really excited and that they wanted to be able to look back twenty years from now and say, "Yeah, I was there for the 1995 revival at Wheaton." I didn't realize the WCF leadership had been so careful about letting the Spirit lead, and not manufacturing things.

I thought to myself that apparently some people must have gone up to show off their spirituality. This made sense to me, because that is how I would probably have felt about going up front for anything.

I had appointments from eight until about ten in the evening, but planned to head over to Pierce to see what was going on after that. Instead, I spent about forty-five minutes discussing the matter with my buddy M——, expressing skepticism about manufacturing revival and examining motives for confession. He agreed and went on to ask why I was going if I wasn't planning to confess. He warned me that I wouldn't necessarily be edified by people talking about their lust and problems with drinking.

With those thoughts in mind, I went over to Pierce. When I walked in, I was flabbergasted by the fact that every seat in the place was taken. I had never seen it so full. I sat in the back on the floor and listened. From eleven until half past one, I did not hear one person confess something that was not a huge problem in my life. I couldn't believe it. There were hundreds of other Wheaton students who struggled with all the things that I struggle with.

I knew, however, that there was no way I should go up there, because that was exactly what I wanted to do. I wanted to go up so that people could surround me, pray for me, pat me on the back, and tell me I was just fine. I wanted the recognition, and I knew that was wrong.

But I was extremely convicted about my sin. I realized I was the worst sinner who has ever lived. The depth of what Christ died for became abundantly clear to me.

I left a little before the meeting broke up because I wanted to clear my head a bit. I went over to some friends' apartment, figuring I would get a chance to discuss this with them and also have some time to sit and write in my DayTimer. I planned to make a list of my sins and, in a symbolic gesture, burn the sheet of paper, thereby casting them from me.

When I arrived there, only one person was still up, but another arrived home from the service about ten minutes later. I had come to the conclusion that all of my sins boiled down to pride and selfishness. I told D—— why I didn't think I should get up there, and he said, "Well, maybe when you get up there, you should confess that." His comment planted the thought in my mind that maybe God did want me to get up there, but I didn't know.

The sin that became very real in my mind was the sin of drunkenness. I had gone to a weekend conference during January and spent an evening with the guy who had taught me to sell books, and a couple of other people. To start the evening off, we jack-knifed a beer. I had never done that before, and it was the beginning of the worst night of my life.

We went to a club where there were several people from other schools hanging out. I walked in and started talking to a buddy from Purdue. He couldn't believe I had come to that particular bar, since I was from Wheaton. It was a very dark and sinful place. I drank a lot of beer—probably ten in two hours. On the way home, I started acting obnoxious and yelling at everyone I saw. Back at the hotel, I made a complete fool of myself talking to a girl who has done a lot of good work for the company over the last several years. I told her I was from Wheaton, and she couldn't believe it. I never did tell her my name.

That night, while I was sitting in Pierce Chapel, I realized what a huge deal that night had been. I hadn't realized before then that I had really sinned that much. I had promised myself that I would never get drunk again but thought it was no big deal. Now I realized I had totally ruined my chance to witness to my friend from Purdue as well as ruined anything that Wheaton College may have stood for in his mind.

I slept in the afternoon on Tuesday, got up in the evening to eat, then went to the meeting at College Church that night. I was really touched by the first person who confessed that night, because the main thing he wanted was for the Holy Spirit to fill him up and give him power to be a light to the world and to withstand the temptations that would come. He read Ephesians 3:14-21, which became the key verses of the week for me. I was so touched by what this guy said because I feel exactly the same way. I just want to have the Spirit touch my life in a way that will make it the best witness it can be for Him in all things.

I sat there for an hour and prayed constantly that God would forgive me for everything, but I didn't feel any peace at all. I prayed for some other people who had confessed up front, then went outside the auditorium to pray. I was sitting there praying when M—— walked up. That he was there kind of surprised me because of some of the skepticism he had voiced the day before, but he sat and talked to me for a long time. We talked about some of the things I had noticed—how not everything that people had confessed edified me, but that edification wasn't necessarily what the Spirit was doing in this movement.

After I was done talking with him, I went and found N——, because he was the person I wanted to confess to. I felt, because I had known him longer than almost anyone else at Wheaton, that possibly he would be able to help me. So I went and found him. We went downstairs, and I told him about the drunkenness. I also told him that my dad had always told me that drinking alcohol had no inherent badness in it, but that losing control and getting drunk did. I told N—— that I felt I had let my dad down. I also told him I felt I had let God down, because I ruined my witness with those who were with me that night. I showed him my list of sins, which included lust and bad thoughts, lies, bad stewardship of money, but most of all pride, greed, and selfishness. Those are the root sins that I have to get over in order to be where I want to be.

I also told him I didn't necessarily feel I should get up front and tell anybody about it—because it would be a sin for me. He said he understood, because that was how he had felt Sunday night, but he said that when God convicted him on Monday night, thoughts of pride in getting up in front of people and making himself look good didn't even enter his head. The fact that I was so concerned about having the right motives was a sign that God was behind my getting up there, he said, as long as the devil didn't receive a single bit of glory through my pride.

We prayed for a while, and since it was after one in the morning, I decided to go home and pray more about what God wanted me to do. So I went home and prayed, and eventually I slept.

The first thing I thought about when I got up Wednesday morning was that I had sinned, and that God wanted me to go up and seek forgiveness of my peers. I was still real concerned about my motives.

In tennis class, I discussed the revival with several other people. I was pretty happy about the Spirit's work at this point, because I could see that it wasn't manufactured, and that the Spirit was the reason most of the people were going up. I was working really hard at not judging people I saw as I walked about campus, but just rejoicing in God's work.

After class, I went down to the school where I had done my student teaching and helped to coach the varsity boys' basketball team. My relationship with the coach had not gone as well as I had hoped. I stopped in to see her, and we had a great conversation about what had happened that semester. I told her I was sorry for having felt like she hated me. I had not realized until much later that she had my best interests at heart, but that I tried her patience with some of the things I did. Some of my mistakes made her life really tough. I made such a mess of her classroom discipline that it took her two weeks to clean it up. After talking with her, I felt so much better about my future as a teacher and the fact that I was still friends with her.

I told her about what was going on at school. She thought it was the funniest thing she ever heard. The Christian school "gettin' religion, gettin' churched!" She is a self-proclaimed agnostic, and I will definitely pray for her until she finds God. I had been so afraid to go see her, and once I went, I felt such a burden lift from me. It was great.

At 9:00 P.M. I went over to the church. I sat over to the side and prayed straight through until the worship started at 9:30. I was still thinking of not going up there until about ten, when Kevin Engel finally asked for those who wished to confess to come forward. I rushed forward, because by this time I felt I could not wait any longer. I felt like a huge balloon was inside me that had to be let out or else my life was going to come to an end.

I almost started weeping right there in front of everybody. I hadn't realized how big this was until I got up there and was speaking in front of literally fifteen hundred people who were all looking at me. I had to stop a couple of times to keep control of my faculties. I confessed my sin of drunkenness and also discussed how I had ruined my witness in that action. I saw two friends sitting in the front row with their hands outstretched toward me, and I could feel their prayers. It was amazing. I absolutely revel in that feeling. I could feel God take me in His arms and squeeze me, telling me how much He loved me. I can't describe that feeling well enough. Language just falls short.

I also confessed my cynical attitude, that I had been skeptical of God's work, that I had judged many people wrongly. I told them that the base sin of all my other sins was pride and selfishness. I got to a stopping point, and I was planning on burning the page on which I wrote all of my transgressions, but I carried it out with me into the hall.

I haven't cried that much since last semester during my father's funeral. I wept all over one of my closest friends. One of the things that I visualized was having a huge group of people around me praying for me. The people around me were so in tune with the ways I was feeling. One of them left me a note afterward, reminding me that the apostle Paul had done a lot worse things than I had, and that God went on to use him in very powerful ways. That made me so happy, because I want God to use me, and I had begun to think that He wasn't going to be able to. I don't know what I was thinking!

God was touching me in a way that I have never felt before. He started right then convicting me about being open to His will even though I have already made some plans for my future. I need to be open to His leading right this second, because He has something for me—I don't know what.

I went back to College Church feeling so good. It was amazing. The rest of that evening kind of swims in my memory. I remember praying with a few different people. It meant a lot to pray with a young man who confessed his pride. At about 2:05 A.M. the last of at least a thousand people came forward and confessed their sins. Kevin Engel came forward and announced that we were going to get together the next night and celebrate what God had done. That really made me happy. I felt euphoric when we praised for about half an hour at the end of that evening.

I got home and felt I had to call my mom and tell her what was happening. So I woke her up and told her. She didn't even know I had ever gotten drunk. She was so happy to hear that revival was going on at Wheaton, because she had been praying for that for several months. I let her go back to sleep and hit the sack myself.

On Thursday I went to class and learned about George Mac-Donald—how he had been broken so many times, yet had gone on to write a ton of books and become the inspiration for C. S. Lewis, a writer who has blessed many people's lives.

I went to the service that night still feeling like everything wasn't settled. I'm certain that God was still trying to say something to me. That night a lot of amazing stories were related during the sharing time, but the one that struck me the most was that of a young man who was just so happy to be a part of this amazing week. He said it was very unusual for so many people to get together and rejoice in their moments of weakness and brokenness.

Later, during the praise time, I was very happy. I felt God in my heart and pure, blissful joy. I think, however, that God was calling me to something more than just pure joy. He wants everyone in the world to experience the joy that so many of us experienced during this past week.

I realized I had set my plans for the next few months and years in such a way that I was no longer willing to let God decide what was going to happen. I decided that if God wants me to go into full-time Christian work, then I will. I need to be willing to do what He wants, and keep my relationship such that I can hear Him when He's talking to me.

Everything that happened last week was not strange at all. It was all very much like the God that I have known all my life. Only recently, however, did I really start to hear His voice and realize who He truly is and what He can do. If God can use what happened to me, and what happened to me wasn't anywhere near out of the ordinary for this place and time, then my whole life will have been worth it. God is so good, so real, so full of mercy, and so powerful that words truly cannot describe what He has done on the campus this week.

From Eating Disorders to Wholeness

My journey to wholeness began in January at a retreat I attended. The last night of the retreat, we had a Communion service, and before we took Communion, our leader asked if anyone would like to confess anything publicly. The meeting went on for about four or five hours, with people confessing everything from pride to deep hatred for their parents. At the beginning of the meeting, I asked God to show me what sins I had in my life that I had not yet confessed to Him. He showed me three areas where I had not allowed Him to enter, and one of those areas really shocked me simply because it had been my lifestyle for the past six years.

Ever since I was fourteen years old, I have had a problem with alternating thoughts of anorexia and food addiction. Even though I was by no means overweight, I started to call myself ugly and began to hate myself as well as my body. By my junior year in high school, I became so obsessed with eating right and exercising that I refused to eat the food my mother cooked, claiming that it had "too many fat grams." My parents became concerned, and soon I was seeing a counselor. I went for about four months and it wasn't doing any good, so I lied my way out of it, telling my parents that I was "cured." My senior year in high school, when I was alone in the house or baby-sitting, I would periodically eat entire half gallons of ice cream or dozens of cookies in one sitting. I would then counteract with eating close to nothing for days.

During my freshman year at Wheaton, I gained about ten pounds, and my summer clothes did not fit as well as they had in the past. So I secretly began a liquid diet. I lost about fifteen pounds in about two months, and then was forced to stop because my stomach simply could not tolerate the shakes any longer. I began to skip breakfast and lunch and sometimes dinner, since I didn't get off work until long after dinnertime. I reasoned that because my job kept me so busy, I didn't have time to eat.

During that summer, I had been experiencing difficulty with my quiet time with the Lord. A close friend asked me once how I was doing spiritually, and I remember telling her, "I feel this physical wall in my heart that keeps me from God. I don't know what it is or why it's there, and I don't know how to get rid of it." I now realize that it was my sinful thoughts and eating habits that were keeping me from a right relationship with Him.

The last thing I want to say about the eating issue is that it's not just the food. It's all the lying that goes on and the arguing with God that occurs. I lied to my parents, to my friends, and to myself. My mom would always ask me if she could make me a lunch before I went to work, but I always told her that I would pick something up there. I never did. I also argued a lot with God, saying, *Look at her! Why didn't you make me with a body like that, God? Why can't I be just ten pounds skinnier?* I now understand that God made me just the way I am, and that while I should take care of my body by not being grossly overweight, I should also be content with what God gave me.

So anyway, back to the January retreat. The whole time I was listening to people confess, the Holy Spirit was convicting me. I felt like standing up and confessing, but each time I was prompted, I talked myself out of it. When the service was over, I ran out of the room and back to my cabin so that I wouldn't have to face anyone and let them know my horrible secret. While lying in bed, I confessed my sin to God and felt forgiven. However, in the next three months, I was attacked more fiercely than I had ever experienced in the past. In Luke 11:24-26, Jesus said,

> *When an evil spirit comes out of a man, it goes through arid places seeking rest and does not find it. Then it says, "I will return to the house I left." When it arrives, it finds the house swept clean and put in order. Then it goes and takes seven other spirits more wicked than itself, and they go in and live there. And the final condition of that man is worse than the first.*

I believe that Satan saw that I was forgiven but still weak, and attacked me further. So by the time God moved in March, I was thoroughly discouraged.

When God chose to touch Wheaton in such a dramatic way on the evening of March 19, 1995, I was absolutely over-whelmed. I stayed for the entire marathon that was the first service. I wept and rejoiced and marveled at how God had allowed me to experience such an outpouring of His Spirit. The first three nights, I really felt led to pray for people and to heal some relationships with friends at school. However, God had other plans for me. When I walked into the service on Wednesday night, March 22, I felt the Holy Spirit prompting me to confess. So I walked up to the front and told my story to fifteen hundred people. When I finished, people prayed over me and I felt the wall between God and me physically go away. I felt so new and whole and forgiven.

During the hours immediately following my confession, I sat in the hallway and talked to one girl after another who struggled with the same thing and who just couldn't seem to come to the place where they could give it up. It was a joy to pray for these girls and to see some come to know the forgiveness that I experienced.

The revival changed the way I interacted with many people, especially with those who struggled with eating disorders. Instead of glibly saying, "Hi! How are you? Good!" and then continuing on my way, I found myself asking and being asked, "Hi, how are you doing today? How are you really feeling?" There were no more walls to contend with, no more facades created by those who didn't want anyone to know who they really were.

My journey to wholeness has not been an easy one, and I have fallen along the way, but there is now a difference. Previously, when I had "messed up," I hated myself even more and grew angrier with God. Now, when I fall, I know that I am forgiven and loved by the Creator of the universe, and there is nothing I can ever do to take His love from me. Also, when I am tempted to fall back into my old lifestyle, I have said, "Get away from me, Satan! You no longer have a hold on me!" Hallelujah! We serve a mighty God!

Public and Private Confessions
Lead to Freedom

On my way to church, I noticed the sign in the stairwell that said something about two students coming to campus to talk about some revival that had happened at their campus, and I thought: *Crimony! I'm not going to be able to go to World Christian Fellowship tonight because of our youth cell group. Well, maybe I will make it back in time to hear them.*

I didn't get back until 9:30 that night, and I was rather annoyed that I had missed all of WCF, as it never goes past 9:30. I went to my room, and about two minutes later, my roommate came in. "How did WCF go tonight?" I asked him.

"Incredible! You have to go see for yourself."

He told me about how students had begun to share and confess sin in front of the group, and I thought, *I have to go.* My struggle with habitual sin always came to the front of my mind whenever

I heard the word *confession,* and I was somewhat afraid to go to the meeting. I was afraid that if I went, God would tell me that I needed to confess my sin. I was skeptical also. *All year long people have been praying for revival,* I thought, *and now two students tell about it at their school and our school goes ballistic. I wonder if people here want revival so much that they may think this is it?*

Nevertheless, I had a feeling I should go to the meeting, though it was getting late and I had homework to do. I was curious, too. When I got there, I imagined walking in and feeling the Holy Spirit just engulf me, but it didn't happen, and I wasn't really surprised. I stood and watched for a bit, then finally convinced myself to sit down somewhere and pray. People were sharing and confessing, but I wasn't there to be a spectator; I was there for some other reason. God knew.

As I prayed, God started the questioning in me. I didn't want to go up to the mic and feed my pride—as if I wanted to confess my sin anyway. I sat there as God asked me about my life, and all I could think about was going back to my room to talk with my roommate. I prayed some more, and then I went up to the front to pray with some friends of mine. We confessed to each other through prayer as we confessed out loud to God.

I went back to my room and asked my roommate if we could talk and if he would hold me accountable. Then I confessed my sin to him.

I felt a change in my life. In the following days, I continued to realize a complete and overwhelming sense of freedom and victory. I knew what it meant to say that I was "more than a conqueror." I knew what it meant to say that Jesus had set me free and had broken the power of sin. Jesus forgave me, healed me, and freed me.

I hadn't been hiding the sin before any of this happened. I had confessed it to God, but it had always remained a part of my life. Now, though, I had confessed it to another, and the prayer with my brother in my dorm room, and the prayer with my brothers on the floor of Pierce Chapel, and the Spirit moving in my heart made me new and different. The rest of the week I attended the meetings when I could, knowing that God's Spirit was on our campus and on our hearts in a way perhaps few people ever have the privilege of seeing.

Jesus has conquered all my sin, and I am a new creation in Him, though Satan tries now and then to dissuade me. He has tempted me numerous times over the past weeks, but the sense of freedom and victory has never left. I say to myself and to my enemy that I am a child of God and have been set free from sin. Satan has no power over me.

I will remember these past few days as long as I live. God has not only set me free from guilt, but He has set me free from the cause of that guilt. He has set me free from the sin itself, and He has given me victory. I wonder now and then if this is a cocky attitude, and if I am going to fall back into the sin. I may make a mistake sometime, but I am not cocky. I have simply accepted the promises Jesus has given me, and I have claimed them as my own. His Spirit has come upon me and is in me even now.

I have come to a new awareness of the power of prayer for our brothers and sisters. I have never felt power in prayer like I did during the week of the meetings. I prayed for people and was prayed for, and God displayed His power. I have become convinced that "the prayer of a righteous man availeth much."

"I pray that out of his glorious riches he may strengthen you with power through his Spirit in your inner being, so that Christ my dwell in your hearts through faith . . . that you may be filled to the measure of all the fullness of God."

Freed from Sexual Struggles

Sunday night I felt a tremendous tugging to go up and confess my habit and struggle with a sexual sin. At some point relatively early in the night, I got out of the pew, shaking, to go stand in line. I could not believe what I was doing. It made no sense.

While I was in line, Kevin invited all the girls struggling with sexual sin to go to a designated spot to pray, share, and confess. It seemed the right thing to do, and the line was so long anyway, so I went up. The love and acceptance of the group was poured out on us with immense force. I cried my eyes out—partially out of pain, but mostly out of joy and disbelief! I had never in my wildest dreams expected to see the day when I would find other Christian women at Wheaton with whom I could share, confide, and relate stuff like this.

I planned to come back the next night, because I didn't feel "complete" without confessing publicly as I had originally intended. As it turned out, I didn't get to confess publicly until Wednesday night. This gave me lots of time to plan what I would say, and in light of the awe we all were feeling at God's holiness, many sins came to mind that I could confess—including sexual sins I know I had been forgiven and even healed of.

Self-consciousness set in, and I became very confused, constantly trying to test my motives and determine just what I should confess. The introductory words of Dr. Litfin, Dr. Dorsett, and the others on Wednesday night were very timely and true, and with a quiet spirit I asked God what He would have me do. *You know,* He gently told me. I finally publicly confessed simply, straight-forwardly, and spontaneously my struggle with one particular sexual sin. I experienced an incredible realization of freedom, victory, peace, acceptance, and great gratitude toward God.

Satan is the deceiver and the confuser. But God blessed me with the *certainty* that I had followed His calling. There is no greater joy than that which comes through obedience in Christ, and nobody could take that away from me. Of course, this was only part of a process I am still going through in experiencing God and growing. Only time will tell, but I really believe I have crossed a certain line and will never quite be the same.

To follow up, I have found several women with whom I have shared and listened extensively, been kept accountable, and exchanged prayers. I believe that the energy I had been wasting for years on self-defeating self-absorption, God has been channeling positively toward Himself. I am so eager to drown myself in the Scriptures, in God, and in the fullness of life that only He can give. I am more excited about all aspects of life, and it runs much deeper than emotion or a spiritual high. The fact that I can experience joy in Christ through both positive and negative emotions is constantly increasing my joy. God is so good! (Rom. 12:1-2).

Healing the Wounds of a Broken Family

I had gone to most of the revival sessions and was planning to go to the last Thursday night session at College Church. I was in my room at about 8:00 P.M., doing homework. The phone rang; it was my dad. I hadn't talked to him in about a month and was surprised to hear from him. We didn't have a very good relationship, so I was not exactly looking forward to talking with him.

My parents had a divorce at the end of my third grade year. This put a huge block in my relationship with my dad. I was only allowed to see him every other weekend and for a few hours on Wednesday nights. We gradually drifted apart. He started to drink more and more. I started to not see or talk to him for months at a time. Neither of my parents are Christians, and they do not really approve of me being a Christian.

My dad began the conversation with small talk. We mainly talked about how I needed to change the oil in my car. He then started to tell me why he really called. He told me that he loved me and wanted to have a relationship with me. He said that losing me was the hardest thing that had ever happened to him. He talked about how he had known me so well when I was younger and how deeply it hurt him that he didn't know who I was anymore. He also told me that he had given up drinking and wanted to get his life back together again.

I think it is awesome that he just happened to call at that time. Our conversation was over at 9:14 P.M., and I left a minute later for College Church, where I got to share my story. Through this and many other things, God has shown me how real and awesome He is. I thank God for all He has blessed me with. To Him be the glory.

A Year of Preparation

This revival cannot be said to have occurred just this week. I began to notice God's preparation of my own life around Spring Break 1994. At this time, God for the first time gave me a clear direction in my life, showing me that He did not want me to be in ROTC. It was then that I heard His call for me to spend more time with Him. I also realized I needed to learn what His love is, what it means, and I needed to learn this lesson in my heart.

The next fall was another step of faith for me. God again gave me direction in my life and told me to follow my passion into a Bible major. This was a lot different from my Physics Education major.

When I came back from Christmas Break, we had a summer ministries retreat where we had a night of confession. During this time, I really felt God at work in my heart, and by the next morning I felt completely set free from my sin. This spirit of renewal continued to happen week in and week out for me. Mainly, this renewal came through Communion after a period of reflection. Then I would go to WCF in the evening and be able to completely praise the Lord again.

Two or three weeks before Spring Break '95, God again blew me away. One week He finally gave me a confirmation to go into missions. Then the revival came and completely blew me out of the water.

When the confessions started and people began sharing their hearts, I soon came to realize that it was my place to pray for the people sharing. When there was the call for all those males who struggled with sexual sins, I went up with a friend of mine who had just confessed, because I too deal a lot with these issues. It breaks my heart to think of how widespread this problem has become. After this, I went straight back to praying for others. By 6:00 in the morning, I was drained.

The next night I assumed my role would be the same; however, I could not focus on what was happening. So I started to do a little introspection and later found myself in line. As I was there in line with the last person before me confessing, God showed me something. I felt totally unprepared to deal with it and still do. He showed me that at the root of all my sins was the fact that I was trying to fill the void of not completely knowing God on my own. He showed me that I used all my friends, family, and everyone else in order to make myself feel better. He showed that I was very selfish, down to the core of my being. He showed that I even *use* Him and the Bible to make me feel better. If serving people is what it took to make others notice and appreciate me, I would do it. This completely broke me. I was totally unprepared for this indictment. I am very thankful for those friends of mine who still loved me unconditionally. I was very sorrowful for all the harm I had done to those who were closest to me. Those I loved the most, I had hurt the most.

I was able to confess to my parents and tell them for the first time with all my heart that I love them. I threw away all my secular CDs and tapes after Thursday night, as I realized what a stumbling block they can be for so many of my brothers and sisters. I also realized, more importantly, that for the first time I could honestly say that I love God. After a year of searching in this area, I finally believed I was on the right track.

Thursday night was just an amazing night for me. I am still in awe of the worship of God that night. That night had to make Him smile. Just to see all of those people who love God pouring their hearts out to Him and praising His mighty name. When I went up for the call for those who are going into full-time service for God, I did not realize how many people there were until after we finished praying. I remember looking back and seeing the aisle packed as tightly as the front was. I remember seeing a lot of my friends standing around me, behind me, and everywhere. I think it was then that I just fell to the floor and praised God. While I was on the floor, I felt that God told me that He was going to do something never seen before with this group. I have no idea what; I just believe God is going to do something amazing as a result of the whole week and all those who went up.

After that evening ended, I was just hanging around talking to some friends. As I was talking with a group, two girls started singing hymns. So I came over and joined them on the stage. After a while, there was a whole group singing whatever hymn we could think of until they turned off the lights on us. That time of singing at the end symbolized a lot for me. People I didn't know gathered together to praise the Lord for His mighty deeds. May the Lord's name be praised forever!

A Basketball Team Transformed

Leading a competitive women's basketball team is a challenge on the court. But I found the off-court competition to be the most challenging, especially when it was between key players.

Competition and rivalry between players for starting positions resulted in interpersonal problems that lasted all through the season. One player hated being at Wheaton and was making plans to transfer. Another was into alcohol. One was using drugs. Another was questioning whether there even was a God. In spite of victories in other areas, the team was struggling internally.

Tensions continued to build throughout the year. On the second night of the campus revival meetings, three of the team members went to the microphone together. Their confessions spilled out. Afterward, other team members rushed forward to pray for the three. That prayer became a turning point for our team.

That same night, one key player went up to another, who she had previously seen as a threat to her position, and said, "Let's start over. I want to be friends." Later that week they were riding on a fourteen-hour road trip and having a wonderful time talking together.

A few nights later, coming to the microphone, another team member announced her new start: "I've been filled with alcohol too long, but I want to be filled with the Holy Spirit." She stuck with it. She's always been sweet, but she's a changed girl.

One of these team members was so committed to her new beginning that she created a Bible reading chart, including a Gospel passage and Proverb to read each day. She copied it for the other players. Weeks later, back in their home states, they still call each other weekly to hold one another accountable.

At the team Bible study, one renewed player read Matthew 5:8, "Blessed are the pure in heart, for they shall see God." She exclaimed, "Hello! Maybe if my heart was pure, then I could see God. We get frustrated because we say that God isn't making Himself real to us. We blame it all on God, while continuing to live a worldly life, consuming ourselves with music, movies, and all the things that are distractions during the day, instead of allowing ourselves to be consumed by the Word and by God."

This is what I think is the bottom line. You have to examine yourself, opening up to allow God to clean you out.

Dealing with Sin Every Day

During my sophomore year, I was really frustrated. God didn't seem real to me. I hang out with three people most of the time, and with them it was exactly the same situation. We were all frustrated and fighting.

My roommate came in at 4:30 in the morning, woke me up, and said there was a lot happening over in Pierce Chapel. She said, "You should go over there tomorrow."

I went the next night, but I was kind of skeptical because I heard people were getting up there and saying a lot of dramatic stuff, but on the other hand, if God was doing something I didn't want to miss it.

But I was skeptical of how accepting the people would actually be and how wise it was to get up there and say those things.

After that, I ended up going to all of the meetings. I had a lot of homework that week, and I kept saying I was just going to stay for the singing part and then take off after a little while, but I always ended up staying the whole time anyway.

My one friend who I was fighting with came over and wanted me to go downstairs and talk to her. So we talked about a lot of our problems and worked it out and apologized.

Then we came back upstairs, and I sat there for about a half hour, feeling like I should go up and confess. Obviously God was telling me to do it, because that's not something I would normally do at all.

After a long inner struggle, I eventually decided that if I followed through with the conviction, God would be faithful to get me through it.

My friend who I had been fighting with came up there with me. I told everyone that my problem this year is that I let Jesus be Savior but not Lord. I put some things up on stage and said that from that day forward I would make Jesus Lord.

After we got done, about fifty people came up to pray for us. They were people I knew from all different places on campus, so that was really good to see. People really just wanted you to get right. They weren't concerned that you did this or that. It made a pretty big impact on us.

Afterwards, I was talking with this guy who was crying and saying that this is what the church should be like. We saw people just loving each other regardless of anything. If church was like that, then who wouldn't want to be a Christian?

It was good for our campus, because there are so many people who have so many problems at Wheaton, and you feel like you're not allowed to have any problems, because you're supposed to be the "cream of the crop."

It wasn't just a one-week thing and then it's over. My friends and I realized what sin is and how it separates people from God and from each other, how serious it is, and how it needs to be dealt with. You wouldn't have to go through these big ordeals if you would just deal with it every day.

That's what I did after that night. I was praying a lot that God would show me other areas of sin that I might not be aware of and to show me people I needed to talk to where relationships were strained. And He did! Over the next three weeks it wasn't a lot of fun, but I was able to get a lot of things right. After the revival, I committed myself every day to dealing with sin and not letting it build up.

Before the revival, when I was frustrated that God didn't seem very real, I realized that if you've got a big wall of sin between you and God, well, no wonder you can't hear Him very well!

We all read the verse in Matthew 5:8, where it says that it is the pure in heart who will see God. If you're going to be pure in heart, you have to deal with your sin.

I remember at one of the WCF meetings after the revival, a lot of people were coming up to tell us about all of the other colleges they had visited. Then we started praying for all those schools.

I started thinking about my brother who isn't a Christian. He had come up with my dad and my younger brother to the last night of the revival. I started thinking about most of my friends at home who are not Christians, and I started crying. For thirty minutes I was sobbing, and I couldn't stop because I kept thinking about how these people are not saved. I ended up praying for them and praying for God to forgive me for hindering His work in their lives. Nothing like that has ever happened to me before!

I had been praying for my brother that whole week. Then my parents called me Friday morning to tell me that he had been saved that Thursday night—just four days after the night I cried and prayed for him. I was pretty amazed!

God Brings Racial Understanding

I came to Wheaton with great expectations. I've never met so many white people who are so nice and really seem like they like me. But I realized that many people who smile at my face or say "Hi" or "You sing wonderfully" did not necessarily like me. This was evident in the revival by some things some people said.

And I really got bitter. I never thought I could be so bitter and so angry with people. One day in my dorm, I said hello to this one girl. She walked right past me and didn't say a word. She walked to the very next room, where there was another young lady who was white. She spoke to her and hugged her, and it was like a big family reunion. And I thought, *Now what was the difference in her not speaking to me?* And my feelings were very hurt.

I've had people tell me, "Wow, you guys have hair like wool," and that kind of stuff is offensive to me.

When the [revival] happened, I was totally open to God in that area. I was looking for healing from some hurts. I was excited that God would bless our campus.

There was a girl who got up and said, "I was bitter toward black people because I thought they were bitter toward me." And that made me think, *Do I act bitter toward people when I walk around campus?* This semester, I had to say yes. I thought, *God, I've been sitting here saying these people do this and that, but I haven't been looking at what I've done to prompt some of their action.* So I had to go back in my life and ask, *What have I done to make her or others feel that I don't like them?* He pointed some things out to me.

After that, I saw her in the dining hall and said, "I appreciate what you said, and I'm sorry if I was ever one of the ones who made you feel like I had something against you."

I mentioned her statement to a couple of friends and said, "Obviously, if she thinks we don't like her, then there's something being done to give her this idea. We need to think about what we do, too," and they agreed.

Uncovering Satan's Lies

I have been made newly aware of the lies and deceit Satan uses to taunt and hurt me as a Christian. Through prayer and listening to wise Christians, I have called many lies for what they are— lies. Two trained friends and I went through the "Seven Steps to Freedom in Christ," by Dr. Neil T. Anderson of Freedom in Christ Ministries, to renounce and break the holds Satan has had on my life, especially through deceit and pride.

The battleground is in my mind. Since I want to serve Christ with my life (a formal declaration I made at the Thursday night meeting) and am quite a reflective person by nature, I am susceptible to believe deceiving thoughts about my spiritual walk. One of the biggest issues has been in my performance as a Christian. It is good to obey the Lord's commandments. Praying, reading the Bible, and confession are all necessary. In small ways, though, I have felt inadequate in doing these things, sometimes even taking pride in noticing my inadequacy. I lived under compulsions and expectations: "I should . . . , I ought to . . . , I feel I must . . . ."

For example, I struggled with public confession during the revival week meetings. I knew in my head that it was not necessary for everyone who sinned to confess (that would be all of us), but I believed that in order to really be forgiven I had to confess publicly. Until I did that, I would not have done enough. That was a lie from the evil one, who lies to torment me with thoughts of inadequacy as a Christian. I have been able to uncover and renounce these lies.

Jesus has called me to know and accept His love. From my heart, I could not understand how such a love could be possible, so I held back from receiving all He had to give me. But His desire is for me to know His love for me that does not depend on what I do or don't do. His love is there regardless of what others think of me or don't think of me. I don't need to perform to receive His love. I have known this fact for years, but now I am learning it in my heart.

Accountability for Lasting Change

I sat in my seat throughout the majority of the confessions, supporting my friends when necessary, a bit confused that I was not being mightily convicted to approach the microphone as so many others had. Surely I was not pure from sin, nor exempt from the commandments of the Bible to confess our sins one to another. Nonetheless, I stayed in my seat.

The following Monday, in my weekly prayer meeting with four other guys from my discipleship small group, the suggestion was made that we become decidedly more serious about our commitment to accountability. After realizing the gravity of such a commitment, we began slowly to open up to each other and share our struggles—all of them.

Our experience was approached cautiously, wanting to make sure that everything that was said and done was biblical and out of love for each other.

After prayer that evening (yet another late night), we set out to change some habits that had previously been changing us. The next week when we met, the meeting had a new flavor that spoke joy, commitment, and a deepened friendship. All had not been flawless that week, but even in my life, improvement had finally raised its head.

The third meeting is tonight, and I am excited to find out what battles have been won this week. God is showing me little by little what corners and not so out-of-the-way places need to be abandoned, slowly so I don't get depressed. I think this will be a longer-lasting change, and I will be better for it. Just when I think I'm doing well, God points at another area that needs work. There seems to be an endless supply of corners in my life—kind of an interesting mathematical phenomenon, but He is patient to continue His work.

False Confession—True Confession

After listening to the confessions for a while, I sensed that I needed to get up and say something if I wanted to leave that chapel any different than I had come in, but I didn't know what I needed to confess—my life seemed to be in pretty good order to me. But as I tried to pray for other people or to take joy in their victory, I felt burdened and overwhelmed by some unknown heavy weight.

By this time, the lines to confess extended all the way back along the sides of the chapel to the back of the room, but I got up and stood in line, waiting for my turn to say something, though I still didn't know what. As I stood in line for more than an hour and the clock moved past midnight, I began to get very cynical and found myself joking and cutting others down as they made their confessions. By the time I got to the front, I didn't really want to be up there anymore but felt I was obligated to say something. That evening I confessed that I am an overly independent person who rarely, if ever, turns to or relies on my brothers in Christ for help when I go through struggles or difficulties. As a result I often expect that others will handle their own problems in a similar way, and I don't make myself available to them as I should.

After I finished, I stepped down and a group of guys immediately surrounded me to pray for me, but even as they did so I felt resentful of the fact that they needed to pray for me, and angry that they were so willing to help me. That night I left the building in a state of inner turmoil, not really sure what I had accomplished, but certain that I had done something fairly important.

The next morning I went to class, and everyone seemed exactly the same as they had the week before; there was no "new atmosphere" on campus, no drastic change in the students, nothing to indicate that what had happened the night before had actually occurred.

Feeling discouraged, but sure that something very real and very good had occurred that night, I delved into Hebrews for my devotions that afternoon. In reading Hebrews 3 and 4 I was truly convicted of my hard heart and stone-cold soul. Paul quotes three separate times from Psalm 95:7-8, where it says, "Today, if you hear his voice, do not harden your hearts," and I realized that God had been speaking and moving in a lot of people that Sunday night, but I had such a hard heart and cynical attitude that I had not been able to hear Him or feel His presence as everyone else seemed to. My brain had captured God in the box of my own experience so that I had not been open to His moving in a different way. I failed to recognize that God was touching people in a much deeper sense than I ever imagined could actually happen in our time and place.

When a friend of mine walked in the room and asked what I was doing, I broke down and confessed these things to him, and he listened, prayed, and encouraged me in my resolution to get back up in front of those people and really confess the sin that ran far beneath that which I had pretended to confess the night before.

That night, the chapel was packed with those who had been there the night before as well as those who were curious as to what was going on. After a time of praise and singing, the opportunity for confession was presented once again, and people began to come forward. After fighting within myself for a few minutes, I walked to the front of the room. When I began to speak, I forgot that these were people I knew listening, and for once in my life I spoke without seeking commendation or praise, but only acceptance, support, and love. That is exactly what I received.

When I stepped down this time and the people came forward to pray for me, I was glad that they came and content to have them pray for me. After we finished praying, I turned to look at these friends who had come to support me and was thankful for their presence. One of them turned to me and said joyfully, "I'm so glad, I'm so glad," and I realized that she had been in front of me in line the night before and had heard all my comments and witnessed my negative attitude, and was overjoyed that I had come around and been able to experience the real truth of the experience.

That night I stayed for more than two hours listening to people, praying for people, and revelling in the love and grace that was so overwhelmingly present in that building. In complete contrast from the previous night, I was able to really feel what was happening and to communicate with my Creator in a much more personal way.

Praying in the Pews

Until revival shook our campus between March 19 and 23, the rest of the student body had never been very real to me. The capacity in which God chose to have me work was praying for others from the pew. Those who went to the front and confessed their deepest, best-hidden sins before the student body or laid stumbling-block objects on the podium needed prayer. Others were called by the Lord to go forward and pray with them after each confession, nearly all of which ended in tears of repentance.

Although I stayed in the pew, I sincerely cried for the first time since I came to Wheaton. Rarely am I deeply emotionally moved, especially to the point of tears. I operate best and most comfortably on the intellectual level. That fact created in me a substantial amount of skepticism before I experienced for myself God's movement on our campus.

Deeply emotional religious displays always seemed like a tidal wave to me—a massive, powerful, all-enveloping rise, and a quick, heavy crash to the sand again, with no lasting effect. However, this was more than emotion. It involved hearts in a spiritual sense—more than just an emotional sense. I felt the deep sincerity of it, the movement of the Lord in the hearts and spirits of His people.

I cried, moved by a grief that gave me a glimpse of the terrible and beautiful sadness that must rend the Lord's heart when He looks down and sees us hurting so badly because of sins we committed and wrong choices we made. Our sins must hurt the Lord so much more because He has a fuller, holier love for the world and the community than I could ever have.

The Thursday night service was a bandaging of the wounds opened during the week. It was a time of victory and a time of praise for the grace God pours out on us so freely like ointment, bathing us with Jesus' blood and purifying us as white as freshly fallen snow. It was a practice for eternity, when as a body, all Christians will glorify the Lord forever. I couldn't stay the whole time, despite the refreshing testimonies and calls to act upon the grace God spilled out so richly on us. There were other obligations involving schoolwork that constituted my present, best submission to God's will.

I thank God for the work of revival He did at Wheaton, and I will never forget it. The glimpse He gave me into the humanity of my brothers and sisters in Christ, the necessity of His grace, and the gloriousness of His all-encompassing love for sinners such as me will remain with me forever.

A Changed Heart

One Friday afternoon I received a phone call from my girlfriend. She sounded excited and said she had a message on her answering machine from a friend from another college. He was going to be in Chicago that weekend and wanted to know if he could come to Wheaton to visit her for a few days. She kindly asked me if it would be okay if he stayed in my room, knowing that I would not have a problem with it, but for some reason something inside me cringed. I was tired and didn't feel like entertaining anyone.

Although I said yes, inside I did not like the idea at all. I apologized for my wrong attitude, and to be honest, I could not understand why my reaction was so negative.

He arrived Saturday night. That night we spent some time talking and getting to know each other, and the more we spoke, the more God began to convict me of my rotten attitude. It was evident that he was hurting inside. We talked a great deal about holiness and many other issues that were bothering him. He expressed that some of the rules at Wheaton, such as the prohibition of smoking, drinking, and dancing, seemed paternalistic and legalistic. His attitude toward drinking and smoking was more permissive, dependent on individual choice.

The next morning in church I prayed especially for him. We had more conversations about the Lord. He seemed frustrated. He was unhappy with school and had lost interest in his classes. Nothing was going the way he wanted it to.

We went to WCF that night. I had no idea who was speaking, but I prayed that God would touch him. Soon after the weeping began and the first few people confessed their sins, someone jumped on the stage and screamed, "I don't understand why this isn't happening at my school. Nothing like this is happening there. Somebody has to do something!" I looked up, and there he stood. He jumped back down to the ground, and those around him laid their hands on him and began to pray.

As time passed and more students confessed, he joined the line, eventually confessing his sin before us all. I was so excited that God had given him another chance. The Lord answered my prayer and the prayers of many others.

Since then I have talked to him once. He found someone at school to pray with and has his desire back for his studies. He now realizes how much God loves him, and he prays continually for his campus. "It's true," he says. "God has changed my heart."

Developing a Sense of Urgency

Since Christmas I had been praying that God would show me any sin in my life that was keeping me from a closer relationship with Him. Of course, my prayers were a bit halfhearted; I didn't really think there was any sin in my life. There was, and God in His infinite mercy showed it to me.

I realized for the first time that I was being poisoned by bitterness that I had held against a friend for more than five years. I experienced reconciliation with my brother and with God about three weeks before God's mighty move on our campus. As a result, I was able to rejoice freely with my brothers and sisters as they experienced the same reconciliation.

I have always imagined that a move of the Holy Spirit such as Wheaton experienced would be a charismatic event. However, in no way would I describe what happened on our campus as "charismatic." It was a beautiful thing to participate as people from a wide range of backgrounds experienced the Holy Spirit.

I have begun to understand humility. When one sees a glimpse of what human beings are in relationship to what God is, he must ask in amazement with the psalmist, "What is man, that Thou art mindful of him?" (Ps. 8:4, KJV). We are dust, yet God loves us and chooses to limit Himself by using us. He promises that if we live in Him, we will bear fruit. That fruit can come from dust is an amazing thing!

"The earth is [God's] footstool" (Isa. 66:1), and Wheaton is a very small place on the earth. What a small glimpse of the Almighty God we must have seen—merely His fingertip!

I was amazed at the pain that was poured out of our hearts during the week of confessions. Never before did I understand the devastation sin brings to our lives. In light of this comprehension, many of Jesus' teachings became incredibly meaningful to me for the first time. "You will know the truth, and the truth will set you free" (John 8:32). Sin truly is slavery, but Jesus has broken our bondage. We can be free! "I am come that [you] might have life, and that [you] might have it more abundantly" (John 10:10). Many of us began living for the first time during this amazing week.

Thursday night was a night of testimony to God's goodness. We recognized the immense grace and mercy of the Lord, and our reaction was corporate. We fell at the feet of our Savior and Redeemer in awe and in joy! Together we sang and praised Him. I have never before experienced such joy. As I left the auditorium I could only think of one thing—we are going to do that for eternity . . . only better!

Many people will never experience the freedom, life, and joy that students on Wheaton's campus have experienced. Some of them are living under the oppression of communism and fascism. Others have been taught to believe a lie—Islam, Hinduism, and other false religions. Two thousand language groups do not even have access to a Bible in their own language. In China, where Christians compose less than half of one percent of the population, there is one Bible for every one thousand believers. Billions of people are going to hell because they have never heard the message of Jesus Christ.

The church has got to develop a sense of urgency as the return of Christ draws near. "The harvest truly is plenteous, but the laborers are few" (Matt 9:37, KJV). I plead with you to support missionaries with your money and letters of encouragement and, most importantly, with your prayers. The strongholds of Satan cannot be torn down unless God's people get down on their knees and pray. I also urge you to examine your heart. Is God calling you into missions? Workers are needed. Will you go?

Open Letters on the Internet

Tuesday, March 21, 1995—Please pray for us here. Please pray that God's Spirit will continue to move in the lives of His people. This is the way it is supposed to be. This is what the Bible talks about. Praise the Lord that He is here and that He is calling His wayward children home. We are all sinners, and Satan wants so badly for us to think that our sins are between us and God alone. But we are a body, and when one part of the body hurts, the whole body hurts. All of our sins affect one another. In God's Word we are called to carry each other's burdens, to confess, to be forgiven, to strengthen each other, and to humble ourselves and pray.

Please pray that we might be able to remain obedient to God's Word. Please pray, as Satan wants to attack anything like this that breaks the bonds that he has on people. Please pray for all the people on this campus who don't know the Savior—that they would come. Please pray for sustaining grace, that this might be a beginning and not an end, that this might be the victory we are promised, and that accountability will be a major part in this community. Please pray that we might continue to be sensitive to God's Spirit and that we don't try to manufacture anything on our own, but that we will be open to however the Spirit moves.

Please pray that we might be able to share elsewhere what God has done and is doing here, that people might be renewed and restored in their relationships to our God. God is doing very genuine things here, but I don't want to try to make it sound glorious and cheery. It is very somber, yet there is a deeper joy. Sin is ugly and nothing to be proud of or to romanticize. People are getting right with God here, and that can be painful and is very difficult.

Friday, March 24, 1995—Since Tuesday we have been meeting every night from 9:30 P.M. until about 2:00 A.M., spending time in public confession, reading of the Word, prayer, and praise of our Lord and Savior Jesus Christ. Amazing things have been happening.

I have always heard stories about how the Spirit has moved and miraculous things have happened, but I have never been in the middle of it. Praise the Lord! People are being reconciled to one another and to their families; there is forgiveness for serious offenses of the past; the hurt that has been a part of so many people has been exposed, and the Lord is bringing healing to people. It is hard to describe what is going on here, but it is so refreshing.

I have been reading in the Bible about how we as Christians are supposed to be genuine about who we are, how we are to confess our sins to one another and bear each other's burdens as the body of Christ. And it is happening. I have been frustrated in the past at how the church often works and how it sometimes seems to be a superficial place, but that is not how it is supposed to be—that is not what Scripture says is supposed to happen. Praise the Lord that the Word of God is being fulfilled.

I have been so excited every night to go to the meetings even though I have been exhausted. Wednesday night the last person who desired to publicly confess stood at the mic. So last night we moved on into another phase. We came together and heard the testimonies of what God has been doing in people's lives. It was amazing. Then we spent amazing time in praise to our Savior, giving Him the glory that only He deserves.

I wish you all could be here to see the Spirit move in this way. Please pray that this won't be the end, but the beginning. Pray for your campuses. Revival can and does happen. God is faithful. Please keep praying for our campus during these next weeks, that we will continue in genuineness and Christian love for one another. God bless all of you.

I have been just overwhelmed with the image of being the clean, pure, spotless bride of Christ. I know that sounds weird being a guy, but it is probably one of the most powerful images

I've ever had. To be the bride of Christ in purity because of His love and sacrifice for us. Hallelujah.

Next week I intend to be back on the Internet as usual, so I hope to catch up with you all. Until then, Praise the Lord!

Tuesday, April 18, 1995—Man, when God changes hearts, there is nothing more amazing to see. Things are still happening here on campus. Hard hearts are being replaced by soft hearts. Praise the Lord! That is a miracle that is definitely as great as the parting of the Red Sea. The human heart has got to be one of the hardest things to change and usually takes years. We've seen people change from one night to another. People changing from hard, rebellious, disrespectful people to soft, sensitive, praying people. It is amazing. I don't believe it can be explained from a human perspective. I am just so thankful for what God is doing.

I want to share with you all a few of the things I have learned from the revival.

I have studied the Bible for four years in college now, and I have grown up in the church. One thing that has always frustrated me is the fact that the church does not seem to be operating like it is supposed to according to the model and standard of Scripture. What I have seen at Wheaton has been so refreshing for me, because it is what Scripture says Christianity is about. It has been such a real, genuine, experience, but it is so much deeper than that. I use the word *refreshing*. It is so much more than that, but neither my vocabulary nor my creativity can go much deeper than that word.

I learned that we as Christians are a body, and no one acts in isolation. Our sin affects the whole community, and there is no such thing as a sin between just me and God. I believe one of the biggest lies Satan would have us believe is that our sin affects only us—that we are hurting only ourselves, and that we act in isolation. "God will forgive us and after all, it's only us we are hurting." That is a lie. If you scrape your hand, the whole body feels the hurt. You cannot skin your knee and only have your knee aware of it. In the same way, all of our sins affect the whole body, not just us. A biblical example is the story of Achan (Joshua 22:20). Sin affects everybody.

I realized a while back that I need to confess my sin. I knew I wasn't called to overcome sin alone, so I decided to confess to an older brother here at Wheaton. I confessed my struggles with lust and other sexual sin and asked that he would pray for me and keep me accountable. I had overcome these sins before by myself, but found myself falling later on and then trying to get out of the sin. I realized that is not how God desires us to be. We need to walk together. There is strength in the body.

When the revival came, I realized that my sin had not only affected me, but had affected the whole community, specifically the community of sisters. I realized that I needed to ask the forgiveness of my sisters, because I had a resentment against women because of the past sin in my life. I hated that sin, and since women were the object of that sin I had built up resentment. I knew I needed their forgiveness, so I asked; and let me tell you, it changed me.

One of the last things that I saw was the freedom of walking in the light. As Christians, we seem to think that believers walk in the light and unbelievers walk in darkness. After all, that's what 1 John says, right? I realized that believers are walking in darkness. When you walk in the light, people can see you from all angles, from all sides, and they can see you well. Everything is exposed in the light.

The Bible says that come Judgment Day, all people will be exposed before one another in the light of Christ, and we will see everybody's sins. Why wait until Judgment Day and be so bound in sin through our whole lives and be so ineffective for Christ? God wants to give us victory now and use us. I don't want to be disappointed on Judgment Day that I hid in darkness my whole life just to be exposed in the end, when I could have walked in the light and been used by God. Christians need to drop our guard and walk in the light, despising the darkness because the darkness kills.

If you need to be reconciled to someone or need to confess your sins to someone, do it. God commands it, and you are not operating in isolation. You are part of the body, and when you hurt, we all hurt.

Some Scriptures that are very important to me as a result of what I've learned are:

> 2 Chronicles 7:14—"If my people, who are called by my name, will humble themselves and pray and seek my face and turn from their wicked ways, then will I hear from heaven and will forgive their sin and will heal their land."

> Galatians 6:2—"Carry each other's burdens, and in this way you will fulfill the law of Christ."

> James 5:16—"Therefore confess your sins to each other and pray for each other so that you may be healed. The prayer of a righteous man is powerful and effective."

> Luke 22:31—"Simon, Simon, Satan has asked to sift you as wheat. But I have prayed for you, Simon, that your faith may not fail. And when you have turned back, strengthen your brothers."

> James 4:7ff.—"Submit yourselves, then, to God. Resist the devil, and he will flee from you. Come near to God and he will come near to you. Wash your hands, you sinners, and purify your hearts, you double-minded. Grieve, mourn and wail. Change your laughter to mourning and your joy to gloom. Humble yourselves before the Lord, and he will lift you up."

Those are just some thoughts that I have had and some things that I have shared. I hope they are as challenging to you as they are to me. Keep the faith, brothers and sisters.

7
The Spreading Blaze

Matt Yarrington

Matt Yarrington is a student leader at Wheaton College in the graduating class of 1996.

When the fire of the Holy Spirit first fell on Wheaton College on March 19, 1995, none of us could have predicted how far it would spread. The blaze raged on campus for five nights, and the hot embers burned on through commencement weekend and beyond.

This outpouring of God's grace neither began on Wheaton's campus nor ended there. The campus revival that erupted in Texas during January spread to Wheaton eight weeks later, but Wheaton was only a part of the massive fire of spiritual renewal going on in the United States. As soon as the news went forth that the Holy Spirit was blessing campuses, calls poured in to Wheaton from colleges, seminaries, churches, and high schools all over the country. At first the college tried to channel all requests through Kevin Engel, assistant to the director of the Office of Christian Outreach. After overseeing the travel plans for approximately fifty requests, Engel had to resort to posting the invitations at his office. Students who were willing to travel then had the opportunity to personally contact the institution and work out the details. By graduation in early May, Wheaton students had gone from coast to coast with the good news.

It is impossible to calculate precisely how many requests arrived, because some came to the chaplain's office, others called the Office of Christian Outreach, and still others went directly to students or faculty. Likewise, it is difficult to know how many students, staff and faculty testified. Suffice it to say that scores of people went out, and many more are still answering invitations.

There really is no adequate way to cover the fascinating story of the spreading flames. The fire keeps on burning. The following accounts are merely a sample of what students have done and are doing to pass the torch as it was passed to us.

Northwestern College, St. Paul, Minnesota

One of the first schools that Wheaton students were invited to was Northwestern College. School officials, hearing of the events at Wheaton, called the Office of Christian Outreach to say that if students could come to speak, they would cancel their planned chapel program for Monday, April 3. Both Elizabeth Simpson and I accepted the invitation. Very early on the third of April, we flew to St. Paul.

As we left the airport, student leaders told us that their campus had already begun to experience spiritual revival. The previous week had been an annual week of special services with Ron Hutchcraft as the speaker. Campus leaders had been surprised to see three hundred students respond to a call for prayer in the front of the chapel. There was weeping and repentance. Other signs were present that this was a special year at Northwestern.

We met with the chaplain of the school and other student leaders for prayer. When chapel started, Dave Spooner, a student leader and Inter-Campus Ministries coordinator, introduced us.

I gave an overview of what had happened during the week of meetings at Wheaton and shared a few highlights of the experience for me. Then I spoke of 1 Peter 4:17, which says, "It is time for judgment to begin with the family of God." I told how three weeks before the revival that verse began to burn in my heart and mind continually, and I didn't know why—until the revival came. I said I believed God has unprecedented things in store for this generation, but that first, before He moves among nonbelievers, He is going to cleanse his own bride, the Church, starting with us.

Elizabeth Simpson then shared some of her experiences during the Wheaton revival. She told how God had dealt with her concerning some long-hidden sin, how He had cleansed her, forgiven her and freed her. Next, she described her awe at seeing for the first time the body of Christ acting as it should. She said, "The body of Christ does not look like you just sitting there in your seats, staring at me while I talk. That's not the body of Christ. The body of Christ is living, moving . . . it is arms and hands reaching out, loving one another, praying for one another. That's the body of Christ!" With great boldness, Elizabeth challenged students to "get in on" what God is doing and learn what it means to be part of the body of Christ.

When we had both spoken, Dave Spooner came to the mic. He had been entrusted by the chaplain to discern what should be done at the end of the speeches. While he is ordinarily a very good communicator, Dave at this point just stared at the ground, shuffled his feet, and said in a monotone: "You all can leave now. Or you can stay. We don't want to concoct anything here, but on the other hand, we don't want to quench the Spirit either if God is working in your heart. So I'm just going to leave the mic open." With that he sat down.

Twelve hundred students were present. We saw only two students in the back get up and leave. After a short pause, students began to walk to the stage to confess their sins at the podium. They filled the chairs on stage, waiting patiently for their turn, and the line began to extend far back in the chapel. Eventually, another mic was set up at the far end of the stage to allow another line to form, so students took turns. Athletes, musicians and every other type of student joined in, pouring out their hearts before their peers. After a couple of the confessions, Dave Spooner asked other students to pray with those confessing. This pattern of confession and prayer continued throughout the day. Sins of every type were confessed, including many sexual sins and sins of bitterness, as students repented and asked for accountability and prayer. Elizabeth observed that "the campus was leveled" by God as every stratum of students became transparent and repentant before God and other believers.

Dave Spooner was present the whole day to help guide the events. At around 2:00 P.M., the student body president, Doug Whitaker, took Elizabeth and me for a late lunch. We gave him some ideas for follow-up for the needs being expressed by students, which he later implemented with the help of administrators, faculty members, and student leaders. We had to leave the meeting, still in progress, at 5:00 P.M. for the airport. The meeting was adjourned at around 8:00 and resumed one hour later for students to continue confession and healing until midnight. The following evening a plenary session was held from 8:00 P.M. until 2:00 A.M., where close to nine hundred students came to continue the confessions.

Northwestern College's president had been in Norway during the events of the week. However, he returned in time for chapel on Friday. At the end of the chapel, student body president Doug Whitaker called on students to tell whether God had done a special work in their hearts that week. He asked everyone present to demonstrate this to those around them, to God, and to President Ericksen by standing to their feet. Nine hundred students immediately stood (Northwestern has around twelve hundred students). Then Doug asked those who had not confessed, but who had been prayer partners for others or supported them, to stand as well. Many more stood, so that campus pastor Kyle Wilson said that only a very few were left in their seats.

In the week that followed, students from Northwestern carried the message of God's work to other churches and colleges in Minnesota and Iowa, with confession of sin resulting.

Asbury College, Wilmore, Kentucky

On that very same day two seniors, Nathan Oates and Stephanie Seidel, left Wheaton early to speak at Asbury College. The week of April 3 was the annual Holiness Week at Asbury, when a special speaker is invited to speak in various meetings from Tuesday through Friday. A special meeting was called for Monday night to hear the Wheaton students.

When they arrived they found a community that seemed "hungry for revival." In the morning, Nate and Stephanie attended chapel, where the evening's special service was announced. Unlike at Wheaton, Nate didn't detect any hesitancy on campus about the word or the idea of revival. Even the table decorations in the cafeteria read, "Pray for Revival."

At 6:20 P.M. Stephanie and Nate met for prayer with Asbury's president, Dr. David Gyertson, the student body president, and other student leaders. There were already thirty people at the chapel who had met to pray for Stephanie and Nate. The board of trustees of the college was also in session that day, but had adjourned in order to attend the evening event.

Between five and six hundred students packed the chapel at 7:00 P.M. Nate recalled feeling a sense of fear, not in speaking before a large group, but because of "the responsibility of trying to articulate what had happened." First Stephanie gave the group an overview of what had happened at Wheaton, recalling the week of March 19th. She then gave her personal testimony of how she was cleansed from past sin during the revival. After sharing for ten minutes, she sat down.

Nate began by mentioning the effects of the revival on Wheaton's campus. He then addressed the question of manipulation, "in order to allay the feeling that we were bringing revival." Nate also mentioned Asbury's holiness roots and John Wesley's belief that "we can be cleansed from the whole power of sin over us." After citing some Scripture, "we just prayed that God would come, and they were so ready."

The student body president next explained that the microphone was open for comment or confession, and people were invited to pray at the altar. Almost immediately, a recent graduate of Asbury went to the mic to confess sin. After him a female student did the same. Stephanie prayed with her, and then Nate prayed with the next young man who confessed. After that, students spontaneously prayed with each person who confessed. Stephanie and Nate prayed with students for an hour, and then sat on the side and prayed. There were occasional words of exhortation by a professor who was a moderator, and an occasional song.

While the chapel remained full throughout the night, many students left and came back as confessions and prayer continued. Asbury's president encouraged students. According to Nate, the sin confessed during that night was "heavy, deep sin," much of it sexual in nature. The meeting lasted until 6:00 A.M.

During the rest of Holiness Week at Asbury, along with the scheduled speaker, there were many meetings that included confessions of sin. By Thursday, the focus of the meetings had shifted to praise as people thanked God for His work in their lives.

Trinity International University, Deerfield, Illinois

In God's providence, the group that was scheduled to speak in chapel at Trinity College on Monday, April 3, canceled with short notice. Consequently, dean of the chapel Hutz Hertzberg invited three people from Wheaton to share what God had done.

Mary Dorsett, Bridgett Mason, and Keith Walker were invited to speak. When they arrived on the Trinity campus, they first met for prayer with the dean and several student leaders. During this time, the student leaders prayed with great expectancy and also began to confess their own sins. They then prayed that God would bring their fellow students to repentance, too.

After some initial singing, Hutz Hertzberg introduced the speakers. Mary began by giving a brief account of the revival week at Wheaton. She compared the events of that week to the heart transplant that a Wheaton professor had recently undergone. Like him, Wheaton College had gotten a new heart, she said.

Then Bridgett provided a personal testimony of how God healed her from emotional wounds. After she spoke, Keith shared how he was experiencing victory over sin since the revival. He then gave a challenge, "Don't wait for any revival to get right with God. Do it as soon as you can." Students were very intent while Bridgett and Keith spoke. No one was asleep.

With five minutes left, Dean Hertzberg invited students to stand and pray. The third person to stand was a student leader who asked permission to speak. After he confessed sin, Hertzberg prayed for him, and then some fifteen students who came to the front prayed over him as well.

After Hertzberg dismissed chapel on time, several students approached him to ask for a chance to meet for confession. That night seventy-five to one hundred students met until after midnight to confess sin and pray for each other.

At the Divinity School, Dr. Robert Coleman had been scheduled to speak at the Tuesday chapel service. However, sensing the significance of God's movement at Wheaton, Coleman asked for Wheaton students to be invited instead.

Dr. Tim Beougher, a graduate of Trinity, was the first to speak. Having studied revivals for fifteen years, he told students and faculty why he was convinced that this movement was a genuine work of God. Next, Pat Bell shared his distress for those at Wheaton who did not get involved in the meetings and so missed out on God's blessing. Third, Leo Sumule, a student from Indonesia whose grandparents were converted by American missionaries, challenged people to take the gospel to the ends of the earth. Cindi Arnold then spoke on the transformation of a women's sports team. Finally, Holly Bell exhorted the group to let God have His way in their lives.

Hertzberg closed the chapel service in prayer. He then said, "Those of you who want or need to leave please do so. We're going to have a time of prayer." Public sharing was not even mentioned as an option, and there were no microphones set up. After perhaps one-third of the students left, people began to stand and pray. Then, as at the undergraduate chapel the previous day, one student came to the front to ask permission to speak publicly. After his confession of sin, students continued to confess sin publicly.

While lines never formed, there was a "steady trickle" of confessions. The meeting continued for several hours into the afternoon. Students also prayed for each person who had confessed as they finished.

That evening three to four hundred college and seminary students and faculty joined together in confession and repentance from 10:00 P.M. until 3:00 A.M. Hertzberg then called on students to fast on Wednesday, beseeching God to continue His work on campus.

On Wednesday, Dr. Erwin Lutzer of the Moody Church was scheduled to speak at both chapels—college and seminary. Sensing the work God was doing, Lutzer spoke on the revival in Canada in the 1970s. "That message proved very timely," stated Hertzberg. On Wednesday night, two to three hundred students, faculty, and staff spent four to six hours in confession, prayer, and celebration of God's grace. Another meeting was held on Thursday night in which approximately one hundred to one hundred fifty people gathered until early morning.

Gordon College, Wenham, Massachusetts

God had already been at work in a special way at Gordon before Wheaton students visited. The previous Wednesday in a normal chapel service, three hundred students had come forward to commit themselves to pray and prepare their hearts for God to move on their campus. That same night at a prayer service, an unprecedented two hundred students gathered until after midnight. These were unusual occurrences. From Sunday until Wednesday, more than twenty students fasted, asking God to touch their campus.

Dr. Beougher, Saranell Kracht, and I were all invited to speak at Gordon that week for special meetings called to bring news about the revival. There was also a weekend conference scheduled for students from around New England, called Beacon '95. While Saranell could not come until Friday, Beougher and I arrived on Wednesday. Brandi Maguire and Chris Robeson from Howard Payne University were also invited to speak. Chris had been present at the beginning of this movement of confession in his church in Brownwood, Texas.

Beougher addressed the Provost Council and then a faculty meeting on the revival movement, giving his perspectives as an historian of revival. At the same time, Chris, Brandi, and I met with the evangelistic drama team led by student Mark Swallow for a time of prayer. At 7:00 P.M. about fifteen faculty and twenty student leaders came together for a light dinner and a time of prayer. This prayer meeting turned into a time of confession as the student leaders confessed their sin and repented before God and each other.

At 10:00 P.M. we went to the scheduled Wednesday night prayer service, where we were supposed to talk. There were between three and four hundred students there. After twenty minutes of worship time, Chris spoke, then Brandi and me. We reported on what we had seen God do at our schools and how we had seen peoples' lives transformed by His power. We also commented on Scriptures having to do with repentance and having our lives restored with God. Afterward, Dean of the Chapel Gary Stratton asked a few of the student leaders who had confessed sin earlier to share what God had done in their lives. As they were speaking, others began to come forward and waited to speak. Students wept as they confessed their sins against God and each other, and others gathered around to pray for each one when they had finished confessing. The meeting had a quietness about it. At 3:00 A.M., with students still waiting to confess, the meeting was adjourned until the following evening.

The next evening, Thursday, four to five hundred students and many faculty and staff came for a continuation of the events. Now, in addition to public confession, there were also times of small-group prayer. Dean Stratton gave an exhortation, and the evening ended with students praying in groups for a fresh infilling of the Holy Spirit. The meeting was dismissed at 2:00 A.M.

Friday night was the beginning of the weekend conference called Beacon '95. John Fischer was the special speaker. He began the conference talking about the need to expose our sins to the Light. When he finished, Saranell and I told the two or three hundred students gathered about the events at Wheaton. Then two Gordon students, including Mark Swallow, spoke on what had occurred there that week. Afterward, students from Gordon College and other New England schools were given the chance to respond. There were confessions of sin as well as updates on the state of affairs at various colleges and universities in the northeast region.

By a "convergence of providence" there was an all-school day of prayer scheduled at Gordon for the following Tuesday. About five hundred students, faculty, and staff gathered voluntarily to pray for awakening at Gordon, in New England, and in the world. At midnight, hundreds of students gathered at a huge bonfire, after the model of Acts 19:19, to throw into the flames items that were hindering their Christian walks. Cassettes, CDs, novels, magazines, sins named on paper, and other items were burned. Students lingered late into the night, singing joyfully.

Eastern Nazarene College, Quincy, Massachusetts

During our New England trip, we traveled to Eastern Nazarene College where chaplain Mike Schutz had invited us to speak. When we arrived, thirty students were at the altar, where they had been all night, praying for God to work mightily in the chapel service.

After a brief introduction, Chris Robeson and Brandi Maguire spoke on the powerful events at their church and college. The chaplain had asked me to conclude and give an invitation for response. But when it was my turn to speak, it was already 10:30 A.M., time for chapel to end. So I said, "I'm going to share some of the exciting things God has been doing at my school. But first, I understand that chapel is over, and some of you have class. You're free to go now." Of the approximately two hundred fifty students present, two left. I then shared about God's powerful work at Wheaton and challenged students to let God do a cleansing work in their lives. After I sat down, students began to come to the microphone in front to confess sins. It was a deep and profound time of repentance. The president, who was in attendance, canceled classes and directed professors to bring their classes to the chapel. The number in the chapel increased as the day continued.

While this meeting was going on, Chris, Brandi, and I were asked to speak to a group of faculty about how they could help students grow in their new-found freedom and deal with their old addictions and sins. The confessional meeting continued until 3:30 P.M., when the chaplain released students to get something to eat. They reconvened at 9:00 P.M.

Cornerstone College, Grand Rapids, Michigan

On the same evening that Beacon '95 was beginning at Gordon College, three Wheaton students were getting ready to speak in Michigan. Yet once again, long before they arrived at the school, God was at work. The week of April 4 was a week of special chapel addresses by evangelist Billy Schneider. At the close of the Thursday chapel, approximately 125 students had gone forward to repent of sins and signify a greater commitment to God.

Saturday night at 7:00 P.M., two hundred of Cornerstone's approximately eight hundred students came to a voluntary meeting to hear three Wheaton students, David Dummitt, Kym Cook, and Joel Dylhoff. College chaplain Tim Cosby explained that after they spoke there would be a question and answer time with an open microphone.

First Kym shared the story of the events at Wheaton, and then Joel gave his testimony of how the revival affected him. David was prepared to speak third, but when his turn came, instead of giving his prepared thoughts he stood and wept in front of the group, deeply feeling their urgent need for repentance and revival.

Chaplain Cosby then opened up the microphone for confession of sin. At first a few, and then a line of students came forward. Spontaneously, other students prayed for those who had testified. Most of the two hundred present responded with confession and prayer, which was "biblical, personal and brief," as requested by the chaplain. In addition, the Cornerstone students asked to pray for the Wheaton students who were going to speak at Hope College the following night. The meeting adjourned at midnight.

At 9:00 P.M. the next night, approximately three hundred Cornerstone students met for more prayer and confession. Students prayed in groups and confessed sin publicly and privately until 2:30 A.M. Monday evening the same scene was repeated, and Tuesday night over fifty men met for a time of prayer and praise. Wednesday night one hundred fifty students met for singing and small-group prayer. Thursday in chapel the president, Dr. Rex Rogers, provided students with a biblical and historical context for understanding spiritual revival, noting that "the Word of God brings a consciousness of sin, the Holy Spirit brings conviction of sin, and our obedience yields confession of sin." The week of meetings was concluded with a praise service in the Good Friday chapel, April 14, where students praised God for the victories in their lives.

Taylor University, Upland, Indiana

The day after students went to Cornerstone, four people from Wheaton visited Taylor University. Erik and Donna Thoennes, Christine Logan, and Bill Merrifield were to attend the final session of the National Student Leadership Conference held annually at Taylor, where student leaders meet from Christian colleges around the nation.

The service was held in Rediger Chapel at 9:00 A.M. Sunday. After praise choruses, the college chaplain gave a short message. Next the conference guests were to share what had been learned during the weekend, and then the Wheaton students were to share briefly.

But when it came time for the conference guests to share, the scene shifted dramatically. The first student to speak was an Asbury student who stood up and talked about the revival that had swept his campus. Another Asbury student then told how the revival changed his life. Next, a few Taylor students stood to speak on how they were experiencing personal revivals. All sharing focused on revival. According to Bill Merrifield, "We figured we could leave, because they didn't need us, but they let us speak. . . . There was confession of sin and prayer and crying and honesty. It was amazing." The meeting continued until after

2:00 P.M. Conference guests returned to their colleges across the country in the afternoon, while Taylor students reconvened at 8:00 P.M. and confessed sin until after 2:00 A.M.

Sunday and Monday there were evening meetings again with confession of sin and healing times of prayer. Alcohol, drugs, tobacco, CDs, and pornography were all trashed. Instead of forming lines, most students would simply wait in their seats or linger in front until there was an opportunity to speak.

On Tuesday the meetings continued and many students came to the microphone to request prayer for a particular country or city that needs the gospel. Subsequently, prayer groups could be seen throughout Rediger Chapel, the foyer, hallways, and stairs.

Wednesday night in Rediger was an evening for praises, testimonies of deliverance, and worship. Hundreds of students packed the chapel, which seats over a thousand people, to praise God for His work at Taylor. After the events of the week, Campus Pastor Chuck Gifford wrote in a memo, "When I hear negativism about what's going on, I'm reminded of being at a football game and having our team score a touchdown. As we all burst into instant shouts of cheer, one somber soul grabs my arm and rebukes my ecstasy with this reminder, 'Don't celebrate too early. There's still plenty of time left to lose!' Well, the confidence we have is that Christ has won!"

Jason Falk, a Taylor senior studying for ministry and a resident assistant, summed up the effects of the week: "People's lives were really changed!" Men who had continually repented and backslidden throughout the year were "turned around, and they've been doing good, you know, until the end of the year! It's incredible!"

Judson College, Elgin, Illinois

While hundreds of students were reconvening in Rediger Chapel at Taylor University to continue their meeting Sunday night, two students, along with several prayer supporters, traveled from

Wheaton to speak at Judson College. Claudia Lopez, who grew up in Elgin, and Eric Sanzone were the two students asked to speak at a voluntary, student-led meeting at 8:00 P.M.

Fewer than a hundred students, but more than the usual number, were in the chapel to hear the Wheaton students. Claudia shared some of the events of the week at Wheaton. Then Eric testified about his former lack of interest in revival and how he had changed his mind after seeing the changes in his and others' lives. Finally, Eric challenged students to be open to the Holy Spirit's work in their own lives.

Student leader Danny Pierson (who was in charge of the meeting) was the first to stand and confess sin. After him a young woman stood, and students prayed for her. While some students continued to confess sins, there were many others who stood to ask for help, prayer, and answers in their attempt to live as Christians. Claudia Lopez commented, "God was doing a lot of unifying, I think, within Judson . . . getting people to break down walls." The meeting continued past 11:00 P.M.

According to Judson's chapel coordinator, Warren Anderson, students continued to meet for two more evenings to confess sin and pray for each other. "People are getting right with each other and with God, and relationships are being changed," wrote Anderson.

Hope College, Holland, Michigan

The same three students who traveled from Wheaton to Corner-stone College arrived the following day (April 9) at Hope College. These three—Kym, Joel, and David—were scheduled to speak in the vespers service called The Gathering at 7:30 P.M. As soon as they stepped onto campus, David reported feeling a "weight of love" for the people at Hope.

Their first meeting was a briefing with the chaplain, Dr. Ben Patterson, and the worship team for the evening. At the prayer time before The Gathering, student leaders seemed to have little expectancy of what God might do at their school. However, by the time they finished prayer, David said, "I came away with the knowledge that God was going to do something." One of the Hope student leaders even commented to his fellow student that there would be plenty of time later to slip away and get something to eat, since he expected a longer meeting than usual.

Students arrived early to pray over the chapel building and anoint it with oil. Kym was the first to speak, telling the seven hundred students gathered about the events at Wheaton. Next Joel gave his testimony of deliverance. A Hope student who happened to have been at Wheaton during the week of meetings also spoke of her experience. Finally, David stood to speak, his heart burning with a concern that he said was definitely supernatural.

David gave the students three reasons why they needed revival. First, because they were hurting. He talked about the many sins in which they were trapped and from which they needed repentance and cleansing. Second, they needed revival because of unsaved students at Hope College. "They [the unsaved] need the church to act like the church so that the church can grow." Finally, they needed revival because some people were offending God with their lifestyles. "Revival is an urgent thing. You are robbing Him of glory because of the way you are conducting your lives and not allowing Him to conduct your lives." David "rebuked them in love" and exhorted them to repent.

Chaplain Patterson opened the microphone for students to respond. Later Patterson wrote:

> I probably went overboard with the disclaimers: "I don't want to manipulate this, or engineer an event, or in any way make anything happen; you can leave now if you want . . . etc." I walked to the steps to descend the platform. . . . Before I got to the floor, students were coming to the mike to confess their sins and share personal burdens.

That was about 9:00 P.M. Confessions and prayer for people who confessed lasted until 2:00 A.M. and continued for the next two evenings from 9:30 P.M. until 2:00 A.M. Confessions included gossip, spiritual laziness, cheating, sexual immorality, rape, abortion, eating disorders, alcohol abuse, broken relationships, and more. After each person confessed, he or she would be "mobbed" by peers who encouraged them and prayed for them. David commented, "It was a marvelous feeling of familiarity— the Lord working in the same way He had worked at other campuses. The Holy Spirit was present."

Patterson later responded to the suggestion of manipulation in a Reformed journal called *Perspectives*. He wrote that the testimonies of the speakers, along with the no-pressure tactics of the event, ruled out coersion: "The meetings were in no way engineered to produce the extraordinary things that occurred. What followed was far more than the sum of the events that led up to it."

Commenting on his own pain at hearing his students' struggles, Patterson wrote, "It seemed, at times, that a whole generation has been sacrificed to Molech. Good Friday, which came later in the week, was never so meaningful. To think that Christ bore all that." Patterson also said that the revival at Hope demonstrated that students are hungry for

> an experience of the church and confession and forgiveness that goes deeper than the cerebral cortex. They don't want a faith that goes against reason, but they do want a faith that goes further. They understand with Pascal that "the heart has reasons which reason does not know."

The fourth and final meeting at Hope took place the following Monday evening, April 17, and was a celebration and commitment service.

The week that followed these meetings was marked by accusations of spiritual abuse from students and faculty who disagreed with the confessional meetings. There were articles in Hope's student newspaper condemning the events as coerced; there were misunderstandings and concern over hysteria and accusations of manipulation. However, in the next issue the paper did not have room to print all of the letters from Hope's student leaders in defense of the revival. Those letters had the effect of bringing a more balanced perspective to the campus about the meetings. The result, according to Patterson, was that by the end of the year there was scarcely a person on Hope's campus who had not heard about it and formed an opinion.

Iowa State University

Kevin Kent, John Chung, and Mark Harbeck drove to Iowa on the weekend of April 9. They gave testimonies in a church where revival broke out. The next day they went to visit the Christian groups at Iowa State University in Ames and to speak at a special meeting on Monday, April 10. On the way, their car broke down, and they arrived with little time before the meeting. Five hundred students from various campus Christian ministries met in a large room in a local auto parts store to hear about God's acts at Wheaton.

After a worship time, John told of their experience the previous day at church. Kevin gave some thoughts on the implications of revival. Mark spoke about how "sin has power when it's not in the light; but when we bring it into the light, God takes care of it." All three also shared their own testimony of change since the revival.

The first person to share when the opportunity was given was a guy struggling with sexual sin. After he shared, one of the Wheaton students invited others struggling with the same type of sin to come forward for prayer. Some one hundred men rose and came to the front for a time of confession and prayer. Afterward, they all got in line to confess and seek prayer and accountability from the other students. Jon Holmsten, another

Wheaton student present, gave a teaching from his notes from the Wheaton seminar "Healing Past Hurts," which offered help for those dealing with sexual sin and hurt. Others confessed a variety of sins and sought prayer.

During part of the evening, John stepped outside for a minute and met two roommates. They had been struggling with many of the same sins and didn't even know it. They were amazed that until now they had not been able to support one another in their struggle against sin.

Another student who confessed to a serious problem with materialism begged those present who were needing funds for missions projects to ask him for money. Later that evening, a Campus Crusade staffer who happened to be sitting next to him turned and said, "Do you have 50 cents for a Coke?" According to John, "The guy pulled out this huge wad of money and said, 'Here, take this from me! Do something with it!'" The staff member later commented, "All I wanted was a Coke!"

Many students brought items of personal defeat, like CDs and clothing, to discard in a garbage bag near the front. At one point, women who had been sexually abused as youths began to speak at the microphone about their hurts. Confessions were halted for a while as the assembly joined in prayer for their healing. Throughout the evening several newer Christians made their first public confession of faith. One said, "You know, I don't think I've ever done this, and I want to do it before you all: I confess, Jesus Christ is my Savior and my Lord!" Some couples also confessed together and asked for accountability in their relationships.

The meeting finally adjourned around 5:00 A.M., with over one hundred fifty students remaining. Tuesday night several groups met on their own for services of worship and praise. John, who has maintained contact with a few friends at Iowa State, reported that the events have done a lot to heighten the unity between the different groups on campus. Also, some groups took the confession motif back to their ministries and continued with more confession where necessary. One of the ISU students said that after praying about it, the students there "don't refer to what happened as 'revival.' They believe it's the beginning of something. They just call it 'The Monday Night.' They think God is preparing them for something big to happen at Iowa State."

George Fox College, Newburg, Oregon

Early on Monday, April 10, Scott Polender and Elizabeth Simpson flew to Portland, Oregon, in response to invitations from two colleges. At George Fox College, where perhaps one-half of the student body profess to be committed Christians, a group of students waited with great anticipation for the visit. Roy Hiebert, a retired staff member of the college and a former missionary who is affectionately called "Grandpa Roy," had been praying for years that God would visit George Fox with a powerful spiritual renewal.

Over a thousand students were in chapel on Monday morning. Elizabeth told the story of the events at Wheaton and also gave her personal testimony of deliverance from past sin. Then Scott talked about several Scripture verses that had become especially meaningful to him during the revival. Then they sat down.

According to Scott, "The chaplain was very careful about not manipulating or forcing people. He did not even want the speakers to invite people to the microphones. He just put the mics in place where people could see them, and people started flying up there."

Lines for confession formed almost immediately after the speakers finished. Students confessed sexual sins, as well as pride and other problems. There was prayer for students who confessed. After approximately ninety minutes of confession, Chaplain Gregg Lamm ended the service with close to fifty students still waiting in line. He decided to reconvene in the evening.

At 8:30 P.M. several hundred students gathered to resume the morning confessions. At first when the microphones were opened, no one spoke. Then a few students rose to pray, while others offered encouragement and a few confessed sin. Near the end of the evening, a female student invited those struggling with sexual sin to come to the front to pray together, and more than thirty students responded. The meeting adjourned at 11:30 P.M. With joy in his heart, Grandpa Roy locked up the building.

In the following weeks, morning accountability groups, men's and women's groups, and special support groups were all formed to assist students in dealing with their new commitments and confessions.

Multnomah School of the Bible, Portland, Oregon

Because the meetings were extended at George Fox College, Elizabeth and Scott weren't able to speak that night at Multnomah School of the Bible. Students at Multnomah had publicized the special meeting on campus, but were not able to publicize the change. So, on Tuesday morning a smaller group of interested students (around fifty) met in a church building near campus to hear the good news.

Elizabeth and Scott shared with them the news from Wheaton and then exhorted the group with a more challenging message: Live completely for God. Several hours of confession resulted, though they were of a different nature than at George Fox. Most students' confessions could be epitomized by the prayer, "Lord, I have not loved you with my whole heart."

Students who attended that meeting later organized opportunities for the wider campus, and several hundred students participated. Eventually, the administration called off school for a day of confession, repentance and prayer.

Timothy Christian High School, Elmhurst, Illinois

Colleges and churches were not the only institutions being reached by the Spirit of God. On Thursday, April 14, two days after Elizabeth and Scott returned from Portland, a special movement of the Holy Spirit occurred at Timothy Christian High School.

Eric Sanzone and Ashley White arrived at Timothy Christian with little expectation for God to move in their short, fifteen-minute speaking slot in the half-hour chapel. They had questions about the openness of the students, and when they arrived, it seemed that only the administrators who invited them had any idea about the revival. The students seemed unaware.

For five minutes, Eric outlined the week at Wheaton, and then Ashley spoke for ten minutes and "laid on the line" their need to confess sin. "Confession is what God demands of us," said Ashley. "If you really want to grow as a Christian, you need to confess your sin—if it is against an individual, then confess to an individual; if against the body, then to the body." Eric feared that she may have been too bold, but then admitted, "I guess that's what we're supposed to give them—the truth!"

The chaplain summarized: "We've been given a challenge here. If any of you want to come forward and respond, you can. If not, we'll just go on with our day." First one guy came up, and then others, for an hour and a half. There were confessions of cheating, lying, gossip, drinking problems, and more, said Eric.

One student confessed publicly, "Mr. ———, your physics class is really hard, and I cheat often." Another came to the front and said, "I don't know if I'm a Christian." Eric and Ashley were able to lead him in a prayer for salvation. As each student confessed, they returned to their seats, where peers and teachers prayed over them.

Moody Bible Institute, Chicago, Illinois

David Martin, president of Student Missions Fellowship (SMF) at Moody, called to ask if Wheaton students would speak in the SMF chapel on April 13. Kate Amerlan, a fellow student at Wheaton, agreed to speak along with me. I gave a summary of the events at Wheaton, and then Kate spoke on the personal changes God had brought to her life during the revival. David Martin then ended the chapel and invited any students to stay who wished to respond in any way. It was the day before Easter break and many students had already left campus, so the chapel was not full. Perhaps three hundred students stayed to confess sin and pray. The meeting continued into the afternoon and was reconvened in the evening. On Monday, after the break, another meeting was held for those who had not been there, and there were further confessions of sin and repentance.

Messiah College, Grantham, Pennsylvania

Thursday, April 20, was the beginning of two significant events at Messiah College. It began the annual chaplain's conference where over fifty Christian college chaplains gathered. It also began a student movement of confession and repentance at Messiah.

Professor Tim Beougher and I flew to Messiah early in the morning. During the day, Beougher spoke with interested faculty regarding the revival movement happening across the nation. Later in the evening he was asked to do the same for the opening session of the chaplain's conference, where, according to Messiah chaplain, Eldon Fry, "their agenda became one of prayer and reporting of awakenings on some of their campuses."

In the evening, some five hundred students filled Grantham Chapel for the weekly meeting of praise, called Powerhouse, to hear Mark Swallow from Gordon College and me tell about the amazing events that had transpired at our respective campuses. Beforehand, seven student leaders and speakers met to pray, and our prayers were ones of expectation and faith. One of the students, Cheri Pinkham, told us that this was the most people she had ever seen at Powerhouse. At 8:30 P.M. the meeting began. After some singing, Mark spoke about the confession and repentance happening at Gordon. Next I did the same regarding the movement at Wheaton, issuing a challenge from Scripture to repent of sin and come clean before God.

Christa Ann Vogel, the student leader of Powerhouse, then stood to say that they would take time to silently reflect on what they had heard. After a minute, one student came to the front to confess sin. Then God came in power to Powerhouse. For the next seven hours a steady stream of students waited to confess sin to God and publicly ask for the community's prayers, help, and forgiveness. All over the room were groups of students praying for one another.

One unusual event occurred during the first confession of sin at the microphone. As a woman began to confess, another woman in the back fell to the floor and began to shriek uncontrollably. While others escorted her to the foyer, I encouraged those present to pray. A few students, unsure of what was happening, left in confusion. A professor then went to pray with the woman in the foyer.

After this, the body continued to move into what I can only describe as a genuine work of the Spirit of God. Powerful heart-felt repentance and healing were going on. The college president was awakened from sleep to attend the service. According to Chaplain Fry, "He was impressed by the level of authenticity and has steadfastly been supportive" of the movement. Throughout the night students left and others filled their places, but the chapel remained full. Wrote Chaplain Fry, "The lives and prayers of thousands of students, staff, and faculty over the years converged in a preparedness for God's handiwork."

The living, moving body of Christ became reality. We assisted Christa Ann during the first hour or so with moderating the meeting, but as she is a very capable leader, Mark and I retired at midnight. The meeting she led lasted until nearly 3:00 A.M.

The days and weeks that followed saw mixed responses from students and faculty, some directly opposing the movement and others strongly defending its validity. The following Thursday, Powerhouse held a follow-up meeting. Christa Ann prepared materials for follow-up which were distributed widely to Messiah students.

Columbia University, New York City, New York

At Columbia University some thirty Christians from different campus groups met in a small room underneath St. Paul's Chapel for an evening meeting. After I shared for less than twenty minutes about the works of God at Wheaton and other places, I quoted a few Scripture verses that had meant a lot to me during those events. Student leaders Brandon Bayne and Reyn Cabrinte then introduced a very informal opportunity for prayer or sharing. Students prayed from where they were sitting on the floor. Then one young man sat in a chair facing the group to confess sin. It was like a family having a family talk. After he confessed, there were those who prayed for him. Then many of the others confessed sin. Often the confessions were between groups of Christians that had alienated one another. There was repentance and restoration of relationships. Others directly reconciled with someone who was there, speaking from the front and asking forgiveness. The meeting concluded around midnight.

University of Wisconsin—Stevens Point

The same day I was visiting Columbia University, four veteran revival speakers drove to the University of Wisconsin at Stevens Point to speak at the closing meeting of Christian Awareness Week. The three men, Kevin Kent, John Chung, and Mark Harbeck, now accustomed to traveling together, asked fellow student Amy Frye to accompany them. The event was sponsored by six campus groups.

More than forty students came, and the speakers focused on 2 Chronicles 7:14. Then a student rose to confess his addiction to lust and pornography. Another student stood after him and challenged the group: "Any guys who haven't struggled with this stand up. That's right. Maybe you didn't hear me. I said, any guys who haven't struggled with this stand up!" Two men stood. John reported that the student said in exhortation: "All the rest of you guys come up here and stand with him!" Repentance and prayer followed.

Because of the small group and the close environment, students felt unrestrained by time. Amy was able to minister to some of the women who confessed to having been hurt by Christian men who couldn't control themselves sexually. The meeting went from 7:00 to 11:00 P.M.

Yale University, New Haven, Connecticut

Two members of the International Church at Yale and I left New York at midnight on Friday and headed for Yale University. At 10:00 P.M. on Saturday, April 22, 150 students packed the small Timothy Dwight Memorial Chapel in the center of Yale University's campus for a monthly Call to Prayer. The Call to Prayer had been envisioned by Paul Maykish, my student host, and others, for the purpose of uniting Christian groups on the campus. A graduate student named Mel led with a few worship songs

and then told everyone the purpose for the evening. His introduction was so well done that it set everyone at ease.

My message began with encouragement at how I had already
seen God at work at Yale. I gave historical perspectives on
Yale's previous awakenings, on Timothy Dwight's presidency
there, and the revival of 1802 (the pinnacle of the Second Great
Awakening). Finally, I challenged everyone to reflect on Scripture (James 5:16 and 1 Peter 4:17). After that, Brandon Bayne
from Columbia University shared some reflections from the
night before, telling how God had moved among the group at his
school. He spoke on sin's isolation and the true meaning of the
unity of the body of Christ. Afterward, Mel got up to say, "That's
all our input tonight. You're free to go, or you're welcome to
stay here as we enter a time of prayer and waiting on the Lord."
As far as is known, no one left.

Several then prayed spontaneously. Next someone privately
informed Mel that he had a dream that when students in Dwight
Chapel were invited to ask for prayer for their hardness of heart,
or "cold hearts toward God," revival had come. So Mel invited
those present who wanted prayer for this to raise their hands. All
over the room, circles of prayer resulted around those who had
raised their hands. This prayer lasted for perhaps forty-five
minutes. Many circles broke into spontaneous confession of sin
within the small groups.

Later, both Brandon and I became convicted that there were
sins that needed to be confessed corporately. After some songs
of worship and refocus, Brandon and I rose to give exhortation.
I said,

> I feel that there may be some of you whom the Holy Spirit is
> convicting of various sins that you need to confess. However,
> some of you may not feel comfortable confessing in this setting
> because these are not your closest friends. But we've got better
> than best friends here tonight. We've got brothers and sisters. I

challenge you not to pass up this opportunity to make things right with God and your brothers and sisters. Instead, take this opportunity. All that will result is that you will be prayed for, and find healing.

There followed perhaps twenty-five heartfelt, broken, and deep public confessions of sins of pride, prejudice, and the need for reconciliation between Christian groups at odds with one another. The whole gamut of sins were confessed.

I am told that the evening's event is unprecedented in the memories of everyone at Yale. Christian groups came together who for many years had resisted interaction. Dwight Chapel had never had a Call to Prayer that drew all the Christian groups on campus. This was a step toward unity. (The previous month, the Call to Prayer had brought only thirty people.)

The meeting spontaneously ended at 2:45 A.M. as students began to lead in worship to God, which was an experience indeed! After that no one dismissed the group. It was as if everyone felt the Holy Spirit had taken complete control and finally the Spirit dismissed us for the evening. Students left in joy.

Trinity Christian College, Palos Heights, Illinois

The next Wednesday, April 26, two freshman girls left Wheaton to respond to yet another invitation. Amara Okoroafor and Kelly Concanon had signed up for a visit to Trinity Christian College in Palos Heights, Illinois. At the InterVarsity group where they spoke, the usual turnout was about twenty people. However, when they arrived, thirty to forty expectant Christians awaited them. The leader of the group told them it was the biggest turnout they had ever had. As the evening continued, more students came, making it about sixty in all.

After some worship songs, a mini-skit, and a special song, the two students were introduced to speak. Amara began by telling about the Wheaton Gospel Choir's own revival during their tour to California in the Spring. She then spoke of the Wheaton revival and gave a personal testimony. Kelly elaborated on what happened during the Wheaton meetings and shared some pertinent Scriptures.

The InterVarsity leader then said, "We're not going to force anything on you, but we're going to allow you to come up if you want to give praises or confessions." She then was the first to do so. Other people followed suit. Amara confirmed, "We didn't do much at all. It was the Spirit."

A Baptist Church in Illinois

Rachel Winn and Ryan Elliot traveled on April 30 to a Baptist church in the Chicago area. When Rachel and Ryan arrived, they found the last three rows of the sanctuary filled up. Nearly everyone was seated in the back! Winn gave a history of the Wheaton meetings and described the national movement of confession. Finally, she reported on her own victory over sin which was a result of the revival. Ryan spoke on the importance of confession in the church and of the importance of not thwarting the Holy Spirit.

When they finished, there was a song. Then a leading deacon of the church rose and came to the front. He was crying, and he asked forgiveness from his wife and the church for sins of lust. Rachel exclaimed, "Afterwards, you should have seen his face. He said, 'I'm free! I've had this problem for seventy years. . . . I'm free!' He was radiant." The next person to stand was the pastor, who also made confession of sin. Then more men rose to confess to bitterness, gossip, and other sins against the body of Christ. Rachel recalled, "Here were grown men hugging each other and crying. It was so amazing! They said they needed a touch from the Holy Spirit, and they got it!"

The service went thirty minutes over the scheduled ending time, something of a miracle in itself, according to some. Rachel reflected on the Spirit's touch among the congregation: "I was overwhelmed by the power the Holy Spirit can have in people's lives. . . . It gave me hope for other churches."

Greenville College, Greenville, Illinois

Even during Wheaton's final exam week, a few students were still traveling to share the story. On Wednesday, May 3, students led a service at Greenville College. Nearly two hundred people (compared to the usual fifty to seventy-five) showed up to hear two students share about God's work. Many students had been praying for revival to visit their campus after hearing of the amazing things happening at schools around the country. Flyers posted around campus read, "Prepare to be Challenged."

Chris Estoll and Rebecca Woo arrived just in time for the beginning of the service. After a song, a student leader prayed expectantly for God to do "great things." Chris gave a personal testimony to the power of confession and its impact on his life. He told them, "I want you to experience the same thing so much." Rebecca spoke passionately about the difference the revival had made in her life, and how God had called students to live at a new level of commitment.

The moderator, a student, then rose to speak: "Now I want us to share what's going on in our lives. . . . I know God is talking to you. So do something." Soon one, and then others went to the microphone to confess sins. Personal sins, addictive disorders, sexual sins, and prejudice were confessed as students embraced and supported one another in prayer. Soon after midnight, the meeting ended, but it reconvened the following two evenings. Many students who confessed made renewed commitments of their faith.

Attempting to Document the Undocumentable

A week after the revival meetings at Wheaton, when students were just beginning to go out and share with other schools, a student remarked to me, "Matt, soon this thing is going to be undocumentable." He was right.

In fact, many students gave reports every week until the end of the school year about speaking at churches and schools. Only God knows the impact those many students have had and will have as they continue to speak to churches, at summer camps, and on local radio and TV shows all across the nation and beyond.

I recently read an e-mail transmission from two missionary kids from Spain who have already spoken in one church and were then asked to speak again at another. Close to ten percent of Wheaton's undergraduates are the children of missionaries overseas. Who can know, let alone document, the work the Spirit of God will accomplish as these young evangelists take the news around the globe?

While the purpose of this chapter has been to follow the spread of the revival from Wheaton College elsewhere, the spirit of confession and repentance has continued to spread from many places as students carry the spark to their churches and other schools.

One student told me that when he visited his family in Minnesota over Easter break, he attended a church where two Crown College students were speaking about the revival that had just taken place on their campus. As they spoke, confession of sin and repentance began during that service. Students from Northwestern College (St. Paul) had taken the spark to Crown College, and Elizabeth Simpson and I had spoken at Northwestern. Similarly, it was two students from Howard Payne University in Texas who came to Wheaton College. And this series of events is only one glimpse of what is happening all over the continent and beyond. This movement of the Holy Spirit is a spreading blaze. It can never be fully documented this side of heaven.

Afterword

Duane Litfin

Duane Litfin is president of Wheaton College.

The phone rang early Monday morning. I assumed it was my secretary with news about the day I had ahead of me, but I was wrong. It was our college chaplain, Steve Kellough. He was calling to inform me of what had taken place the previous night on campus. Sounding tired but excited, Steve poured out to me the details of what had transpired.

Immediately I sensed that we had hold of something very important here, or more accurately, were in the grasp of something very important. But what was it, and how were we to respond? In all my years of ministry as a professor, pastor, and now president, I had known many times of revival, but I never experienced anything quite like what Steve had described. During the previous year I had prayed numerous times for spiritual refreshment on campus, especially with several students who were burdened to see revival at Wheaton. Had the Lord answered these and similar prayers? Was this to be another of the historic

Wheaton awakenings? And if so, what did this development now require of me as president?

The immediate details were well under control, of course, so in a sense there was nothing for me to do. The previous evening had enjoyed excellent leadership, from both students and staff, and Steve informed me of the plans for chapel that morning. Then he explained that there was to be a continuation of the meeting that evening, to give students who had not had an opportunity to participate in a renewed chance to deal publicly with whatever the Lord had put on their hearts. Steve and the other staff members were doing their usual excellent job, as were the student leaders.

But the question of my role did not concern the immediate details; none of these depended on me. I was concerned about the broader issue of presidential influence. How could I best support and encourage, but not get in the way of, what God appeared to be doing on Wheaton's campus? I had not initiated this revival and had no intention of wading in and trying to wrest control of it. Clearly, it did not depend upon me. Yet I wanted to lend it my support. What was the right balance?

Oddly, the question of "getting in the way of" was what loomed large for me. Perhaps I need not have worried, but I have learned over the years that anything having to do with the human spirit is a fragile thing. It was C. S. Lewis, I believe, who distinguished between a fellow enjoying a beautiful sunset, and the fellow sitting next to him enjoying *the image* of himself enjoying a beautiful sunset. The two appear outwardly the same, but the one is engrossed in the sunset, the other in himself. And the distance between the two is desperately short. How quickly we slip from the one to the other.

Should I attend the Monday night session to show my support? Or would the presence of the president deflect even a single student from focusing on what God was doing in his or her life, to how he or she might look in the process? The chance was too large to take. During chapel that morning I decided that

I would not attend the evening session. I would just let it happen and stay out of the way. In fact, it was not until the fourth evening, Wednesday night, that I finally felt the freedom to show up. Since Monday morning I had been praying, counseling with individuals, receiving regular updates, and working with our staff to ensure that we were not leaving anything needful undone. But now I was to observe the phenomenon for myself.

The meetings have been well described in this book and I need not add much of my own detail here. It is enough to say that what I observed there was real, powerful, and of the Lord. I had been blessed already that week by seeing God's hand moving in our midst, but not until this Wednesday night meeting did I fully appreciate the dimensions of what was happening. The College Church was packed with fifteen hundred students, and the presence of the Spirit of God was palpable. It was a moving experience.

But if I am honest, I must say that it was not for me an entirely positive experience. I was distressed by several aspects of what was happening. I found the level of self-disclosure in the confessions to be extraordinary—very healthy were the audience a small coterie of close Christian friends or a pastor, but with fifteen hundred people, many of whom were strangers? Self-disclosure and the ability to trust must usually be proportionate; would some of these students come to regret this level of honesty before such a large group? And could the listeners handle what they were being entrusted with? A group of young men who have confessed to lust, combined with, say, a young woman confessing her own sexual sin, is, after all, a volatile mix. As always in times of revival, what we were observing was a blend of the Spirit-led, the immature, and the fleshly. I knew better than to expect anything else, but I was troubled nonetheless.

But mostly I was distressed by the sheer level of need I observed. I confess that as I sat there listening and praying, and with the awareness that this was the *fourth* night of this, I began to feel overwhelmed by the responsibility of reaching out somehow in a pastoral way to these hundreds of students who were so broken before God and their fellow students. We simply were not equipped to handle this level of need. Thus each new confession came to appear to me, paradoxically, like a new burden, laying its weight ultimately on my shoulders. I felt as though I was being weighed down in the pew by the sheer accumulation of need. Obviously, I was experiencing my own bit of spiritual warfare. But God was there to meet my need too, and to remind me that He is quite capable of transcending the whole and making something good of the messiness that His creatures create.

I was sitting near the end of a pew. Suddenly a young man appeared and knelt before me. With someone speaking at the microphone, and several clumps of students arrayed around the front of the auditorium praying with those who had already finished speaking, this second-year student somewhat nervously whispered to me that he had sensed the Spirit of God prompting him to come over and offer to pray for me if I had any needs. And then, having been obedient, but understandably desirous of getting the ordeal of confronting the president over with, he started to get up and said, "I'll be right over here if you need me."

I put my hand on his shoulder and asked him to stay. I told him briefly of the sense of burden I was experiencing and asked him to pray for me, and so he did. Starting somewhat hesitatingly, he prayed, "Lord, I don't even know how to pray for Dr. Litfin." But very quickly he moved off into what I sensed was a very powerful prayer, in the midst of which he said, "And Lord, I ask that you would enable Dr. Litfin to see each of these confessions, not as a burden, but as a gift from you." And immediately his prayer was answered. I was flooded by a sense of peace about what was happening that has not subsided yet. I could not control what was happening and should not try. The messiness of it was inevitable—such things will never be neat and tidy. But God was in it and I was to keep my focus on him, just like everyone else. We were to give the task our best effort, but in the end He would meet the needs of these students in His own way.

On Thursday night I returned to experience the crescendo of the week. It was a time, not of confession now, but of praise and song and testimony and commitment. God had done something powerful in our midst and we wanted to acknowledge it and give thanks and move out onto a new plateau of fellowship and obedience.

Matt Yarrington has movingly recounted in this book how God used our time of refreshment in the lives of others, and I can testify that for the remainder of the semester there was a new spirit on campus. The follow-up efforts were intense and multi-faceted. Our faculty and staff did a wonderful job of providing help to the students, and our small group discipleship ministry, already strong, became even more potent. Indeed, the final meeting of the World Christian Fellowship (WCF) on the last Sunday of the semester was an electric time of worship and commitment, as students prepared to take their new-found commitment home and, quite literally, around the world. As I write, it remains to be seen what the new school year will bring, but this much I know: God has marked our campus in a permanent way, to both our delight and our surprise.

During that final WCF meeting, someone made reference to the "Wheaton revival." It was a passing reference, but the student who was leading the meeting, Matt Yarrington, picked up on it and very gently urged us all to avoid seeing what had happened here as the "Wheaton revival." This did not belong to Wheaton, he reminded us; we were merely privileged to be a small part of something God was doing that was much larger than Wheaton College.

I pray that Matt was right, and that this book may be among the instruments God uses to spread His fire.